ANTHOLOGY OF TRADITIONAL
YORKSHIRE RECIPES
&
MISCELLANEOUS HOUSEHOLD HINTS

By

MAGDALENA GORRELL GUIMARAENS

Copyright © 2021 by Magdalena Gorrell Guimaraens.

All rights reserved. No part of this publication may be reproduced, distributed, or transmitted in any form or by any means, including photocopying, recording, or other electronic or mechanical methods, without the prior written permission of the author, except in the case of brief quotations embodied in critical reviews and certain other noncommercial uses permitted by copyright law.

Compiled in 2000 by Magdalena Gorrell Jaén Guimaraens. Re-edited, partly abridged and annotated, in January 2021.

Cover flower illustration downloaded from dreamstime.com/stock-photos, with permission.

When a recipe can be attributed to a specific Yorksgen submitter, their name is given below the name of the recipe. Quite a few recipes were sent in without details of the submitter and others came from anonymous ancient family notebooks or cookbooks, several from the 1900s or earlier.

Printed in the United States of America.

Library of Congress Control Number: 2021942341

ISBN	Paperback	978-1-64803-936-2
	eBook	978-1-64803-937-9

Westwood Books Publishing LLC
11416 SW Aventino Drive
Port Saint Lucie, FL 34987

www.westwoodbookspublishing.com

BACKGROUND TO THIS ANTHOLOGY

Family History

In what young people today probably consider the Dark Ages of the everyday use of the Internet, before the dawn of the 21st century, most amateur genealogists such as myself, intent with discovering details of their family history, had to resort to searching in attics through stacks of dusty boxes full of family documents, photographs and letters, examining Family Bibles for details of names, births, marriages, deaths, christenings and coaxing elderly relatives to delve into their memories. Large family reunions were often a godsend as a source of information.

The more knowledgeable and luckier researchers may have already inherited studies and reports from older relatives who were able to consult the invaluable archives of the Mormon Church and occasional local genealogical group files in their town halls and libraries, or in formal genealogical societies as the New England Genealogical Society in Boston, the oldest one in the United States.

It was a painstaking business as every detail had to be noted in writing, family trees designed, details and dates checked and re-checked, especially if one's research appeared to indicate the presence of one or more carefully concealed "skeletons"!

But why this interest in one's Family History? Why these determined searches to discover one's roots? Where was our family from? Why did they leave their homeland? What hardships did they have to endure to arrive to a new country, to a new home? How successful were they? What were their interests? Why is it that this or that individual is especially interested in History? is a gifted musician? a brilliant scientist? a born farmer, or weaver, or mason, or carpenter? Is this something that ran/runs in the family? Why are some of us blonde with blue eyes, other brunettes with brown eyes, or redheads? All in the same family? Why are some of us short, tall, chunky, or skinny? Does that have something to do with what we and our parents, and grandparents, ate and still eat today?

The World Wide Web and RootsWeb

The advent of the World Wide Web brought an absolute revolution to amateur Family History researchers such as I. When we finally managed to figure out how the Internet worked (most of us were not real spring chickens), we encountered a world that truly represented hands across the seas. By now, so many of us knew that our family's roots originated in many different countries across the seas, as our ancestors left homelands for a new life elsewhere. Now, we had a medium that enabled us to communicate with other like-minded researchers all over the world, at the click of a keyboard – (as long as we had a good Internet connection, of course!).

In 1993, Brian Leverich and Karen Isaacson founded RootsWeb in Utah, the oldest free online community genealogy research website. Researchers in the USA were able to research Yorkshire ancestors; second and third generations in Canada could go back to the United Kingdom; Australians and New Zealanders found their roots in England. No longer were we restricted to the availability of a Mormon Church history site near our residences.

When RootsWeb was acquired by Ancestry in June 2000, it provided a huge accumulation of information and thousands of source citations. Rootsweb has been described as always being the "go-to-place for specialized and very complete research information" as so it continued until it was discontinued in early 2020.

In my experience, perhaps the most important feature of RootsWeb was its creation of free, bespoke genealogy Mailing Lists that addressed the interests of individual places and, most especially, surnames within a specific location.

One such mailing list was the Yorksgen Mailing List, originally owned by Denise Oyston, supported by Colin Hinson and the wonderful Genuki pages, dedicated to the culture, past and present of Yorkshire, as discussed with great verve and interest by the multitude of Yorksgen's members, all over the world, thanks to the World Wide Web.

Yorksgen 2000

I joined Yorksgen around 1995 and quickly learnt how to work the Internet as I entered into an amazing exchange with fellow Yorksgeners all over the world. From Portugal, I "talked" and made close friends all over the world – Canada, Australia, New Zealand, Germany, the USA, myself from Portugal, and especially the locals in Yorkshire!

Travel in those days seems to have been more accessible as I recall annual week-long meetings of Yorksgeners in York, where we came from all over the world during the summer months, often renting student rooms at York University. We would meet for talks and conferences by specialists, get together in groups in rental cars to go off and research special neighbouring town records, to the Borthwick Institute, to visit historical sites in Yorkshire, to explore York… It was absolutely fantastic.

When Trischa Jackson, Yorksgen member in Australia, suggested celebrating the new century with a Genealogy Reunion in 2020 in York, the idea caught on like wildfire.

The 2000 Yorksgen Cookbook

I had established a close friendship with another Yorksgener, June Ridsdale in Vancouver, British Columbia, especially when discussing Yorkshire recipes, a subject warmly encouraged by my Yorkshire mother-in-law. Already, there was a lengthy thread on the list as members submitted and exchanged a plethora of family recipes, many of which recreated long-remembered foods from their childhoods. It occurred to me that it might be a good idea to celebrate the event with a compilation of recipes submitted to the list. June warmly supported the idea and together we searched and researched the Yorksgen files, collecting recipes submitted to the page by its members. We posted the idea and contributions quickly flowed in fast and furiously, accompanied with all sorts of trivia, bits of dialect and historical lore, all special to Yorkshire.

Not all the recipes that were sent in were exact traditional recipes, in that many were adapted over the years to the needs of the families, especially those who travelled far from Yorkshire, across the seas to foreign lands. Other, newer recipes, formed the basis of new family traditions. Weights and measures varied according to those used where the ex-Yorkshire submitter now lived, namely Canada, USA and Australia. Of note is that in Yorkshire, cooks weigh solid ingredients, whilst in the USA and Canada, these are often measured in cups as are liquids. At the end of this booklet, a weights and measures section helps convert these.

I took it upon myself to sort the recipes, assemble the pages and print the book. June was a superb editor and her contribution to the layout and to choosing and referencing the many contributors who freely agreed to be included in this celebration pamphlet.

EPILOGUE

Today, twenty years hence and after a difficult and most disconcerting year, Yorksgen as a mailing list is no longer active and many of its original members have gone on to greener pastures. In clearing out my office on a cold, rainy day, I came across a copy of the original 2000 Yorksgen Cookbook and realized that the time had come to pay tribute to my "co-conspirator" June, who sadly died shortly after I visited her in her home in Vancouver in 2002, and most especially, to all the original Yorksgeners, the many friends I made and fondly remember. Thanks to all their hard work and research, their heirs will find it easier to answer the question: "Where do we come from?" that so plagued us in our youth.

There are several excellent genealogical research sites on the Internet – Heritage, Ancestry, GeneAll and others – and they all cooperate with each other. I, however, am still more attached to FamilySearch, the free of charge genealogy resources provided by the Church of Jesus Christ of Latter-day Saints (Mormon Church), to help everyone around the world to discover their heritage and connect with members of their family.

As you peruse the old and new traditional recipes, the tidbits and the historical sketches in this booklet, many of you may remember stories from your childhood and pass them on yourselves. Maybe, you might even be enticed to try your hand at making a Spotted Dick or a Steamed Pudding or one of the many ways of serving a grand Yorkshire Pudding!

Magdalena
Vila Nova de Cerveira, Portugal
January, 2021

Dedication from the 2000 cookbook:

A Nostalgic Tribute

To our hardy ancestors who of necessity were more than frugal!

Not a particle of any animal was wasted, but afforded yet another tasty, healthy morsel for the table. The recipes for Brawn, Pig's Trotters, Tripe, Bag, Udder, Cow's Heel, etc., were all a tribute to our dear Great Grannies who nourished their families on nearly non-existing budgets.

By no means all of the recipes herein are so archaic. Many of the recipes which were contributed are modern variations of the old and have been either developed or adapted by their descendants, both in England and across the world. The modern cook will find many things to tempt them to try some of this great cookery!"

TABLE OF CONTENTS

Recipes

Biscuits and Crumpets 11
Bread 17
Breakfast 21
Assorted Brews 23
Cakes and Pastries 33
Fish Dishes. 41
Meat Dishes 45
Pickles and Sauces Pickles. 57
Preserves and Jams 59
Puddings and Desserts 63
Savouries 69
Soup 77
Sweets, Candies & Other Goodies. 79
Yorkshire Pudding 83
Wartime Tasties 87

Curiosities from Bygone Days. 93
Hints for the Homemaker. 99
Remedies 103
INDEX 107
Weights & Measures 113

BISCUITS AND CRUMPETS

BRANDY SNAPS
Susan Cook, Westbank, B.C.

The sale of sweetmeats at Fairs is a common occurrence, but brandy snaps are particularly associated with Hull. This Fair dates back to 1279 when the town was called Wyke. The name was not changed until 1293 when it was named Kingston-on-Hull by Edward I, Hull Fair was originally established for the sale of horses, cattle and foreign goods, but soon the provision of amusement became an integral part of the gatherings and brandy snaps were looked upon as a favourite delicacy.

These have been a traditional sweetmeat on sale at Hull Fair for many years. Bruce Guimaraens says the brandy was originally probably imported from Holland.

2 oz flour
2 oz sugar
2 oz butter or margarine
2 Tbsp golden syrup
1 level tsp ground ginger
¼ tsp grated lemon rind
1 tsp brandy

Melt the fat, sugar and syrup in a pan. Remove from heat and add other ingredients and mix well.

Drop in teaspoonfuls on a greased baking sheet at least 3 in apart as they will spread during cooking.

Bake in a moderate over 7-10 min until golden brown.

Remove from oven and allow to stand a moment on top of the stove until the biscuits can be easily lifted off with a knife. Roll the warm biscuits around a wooden spoon handle and leave a minute to set.

CREAM CRACKER BISCUITS
Martyn Gleaden, Wath-Upon-Dearne
(From a 1900 notebook by Mary Duckett, with kind permission from the Duckett family in Sykehouse)

½ lb flour
2 oz lard
Milk
a little salt

Make into a paste with milk. Roll out and cut into squares being careful to prick them with a fork before putting into the oven. Bake until crisp.

CRUMPETS
Christina Flanigan, California

8 oz flour
½ tsp salt
½ oz yeast
½ oz sugar
½ pint milk/water mix
pinch of bicarbonate of soda

Warm the flour and mix with the salt. Cream yeast with sugar, add to the warmed milk/water and mix with flour to consistency of a soft batter. Cover & leave to rise for 30-45 min.

Dissolve the soda in 1 tsp warm water, add to the mixture, beating well, and allow to rise again for 30 min. Grease a griddle, heavy frying pan or electric fryer heat to fairly hot.

Grease pikelet rings or large plain cutters (3-4 in). Place on griddle and pour in enough batter to a depth of ¼ inch. When top is set and bubbles burst, turn and cook the other side. Serve hot with butter.

GINGER BISCUITS
Martyn Gleaden, Wath-Upon-Dearne

1 Tbsp golden syrup
4 oz butter
6 oz self-rising flour
3 oz loaf sugar
1 heaping tsp ground ginger
pinch of salt

Put syrup and butter in a pan and melt gently. Add flour, sugar, ginger and salt sieved together. Grease a baking tray and space out teaspoons of the mixture. Press with a fork to mark. Bake for approximately 12 min at about 375°F.

GRAVEL PATH or SCRUNCH
Kathleen Allott Guimaraens
ex-Rotherham, now Northern Portugal

4 oz self-rising flour
4 oz golden syrup
4 oz oatmeal
4 oz brown sugar
4 oz butter or margarine
1 egg
4 Tbsp milk
1-2 tsp cinnamon or nutmeg
pinch of salt

Mix spices, flour, salt and oat-meal in a bowl. Melt syrup, butter and sugar together in a saucepan over a slow heat. Add to the flour.

Add egg and milk. Beat well and pour into a greased and lined tin. Heat over to 325°F and bake for 1 hour. When cool, turn out and cut into strips.

NON-SWEET TEA CAKES
Christina Flanigan, California

1 lb flour
1 tsp salt
2 level tsp bicarbonate of soda
2 level tsp cream of tartar
½ pint sour milk
2 oz lard

Sift the flour and salt and rub in the fat. Add the soda and tartar, making quite sure that all lumps are sifted out. Mix in the milk to form a light spongy dough.

Shape into small round teacakes (or scones) and bake on a greased baking sheet in a 425-450°F oven. Makes 1 dozen.

ORMSKIRK GINGERBREAD
Mary Cooke, Ontario

3 lbs flour
1 lb brown sugar
6 oz candied peel
1 lb butter
1 ½ lb syrup
1 oz ground ginger

Mix dry ingredients well together. Warm the syrup and butter together. With a wooden spoon work butter and treacle into mixture until a smooth paste is formed.

Drop mixture by spoonful on wafer paper. Bake in rather slow oven for 10-30 minutes.

POTATO CAKES
Christina Flanigan, California

1 lb cold mashed potatoes
1 oz butter
6 oz plain flour
salt

Sift or mesh the potato until very smooth and mix well with melted butter and salt. (Amount of salt depends on how much you added with the cooking.) Work in as much flour into the mixture as it will take up. Form into cakes about the size of a muffin.

Place on a baking sheet or a hot griddle and cook for about 3 minutes per side.

Serve hot, split and slather with butter.

PARKIN

A moist ginger cake usually served cut in squares. It originated in Yorkshire, where oatmeal is always used in its preparation.

PARKIN (1)
Cheryl Hodges

½ lb flour
½ lb medium oatmeal
¼ lb soft brown sugar
½ tsp ginger
1 egg
8 oz treacle
4 oz lard
¼ pint milk
½ tsp bicarbonate of soda

Mix together the flour, oatmeal and ginger Then melt the sugar, lard and treacle and add a little of the milk and well beaten egg. Put the mixture into the flour and mix to stiff batter. Add the soda dissolved in the rest of the milk Mix well.

Pour into a shallow pan 11 in x 9 in x 2 in. Bake 1 hour until firm, in a moderate over.

PARKIN (2)
Mary Cooke, Ontario

1 lb Scotch oatmeal
4 oz butter
¼ oz ground ginger
1 lb golden syrup
2 oz sugar
1 tsp baking powder
a little milk

Melt butter in syrup, add dry ingredient and mix thoroughly. Bake about 1 hour,

PARKIN (3)
Susan Wragg Reddy
ex-Sheffield, now New Jersey

4 oz lard or margarine
4 oz golden syrup
4 oz black treacle
4 oz sugar
8 oz plain flour
8 oz medium oatmeal
pinch of salt
4 tsp ground ginger
2 tsp ground cinnamon
1 tsp bicarbonate of soda
1 egg

Heat the oven to 300°F/Gas Mark I. Melt the fat. Add syrup, treacle and sugar and warm over a very low hear till the sugar begins to dissolve.

Avoid overheating the mixture, keeping the saucepan warm rather than hot.

Sieve the dry ingredients, make a well in the centre and gradually beat in the liquid from the saucepan and the beaten egg. Mix to a soft consistency, adding a little milk if required.

Pour into a greased flat tin so that the mixture is 1 inch in depth. Bake for 1 hour in a cool over (300°F or Mark 1) and partly cool it in the tin. Turn out to finish cooking. If in doubt bake for 5 min less – it tastes awful if burnt! Serve cut into squares.

Note: If you can't find black treacle, use molasses – it's similar. Golden syrup is also good and so is pancake syrup, probably the closest thing to golden syrup in the USA, although made from corn syrup instead of cane sugar

PARKIN (4)

1 lb fine oatmeal
½ tsp bicarbonate of soda
1 lb dark treacle
1 Tbsp demerara sugar
¼ lb butter
1 Tbsp milk
½ oz ground ginger

Rub butter into oatmeal, add ginger and sugar. Melt treacle Dissolve soda in milk. Mix everything together.

Line a baking tin with well greased paper and pour in mixture

Bake in a low to moderate oven for ½ to ¾ hour. Test with toothpick to see if done.

ABOUT YORKSHIRE PARKIN

Parkin, eaten during November and especially Guy Fawkes Night, has been a tradition in the West Riding for a very long time. What the significance of this practice is, is difficult to know. It is known, however, that a similar cake is made in Lancashire by the name of Hardcake or "soul mass cake" and is also traditionally associated with November and particularly with All Souls' Day on November 2nd. "Har" is the Norman name for Odin, so there may perhaps be a pagan origin. Some authorities say that the soul mass cakes may have been placed on the graves of the departed so that they would not go hungry in after life.

Susan Cook

SCONES

Scone may be pronounced to rhyme with Ron, phone, or moon! Whichever, they all taste the same!

"My four following recipes for scones are from Evan's Recipe Cookery Book (more than 100 years old). I have not tried any of these recipes. Hope someone out there has had a scratch cook for a mother as often quantities are not given (i,e, milk in the following recipe) and oven temperatures must be for wood burning ovens as degrees C or F are not given."

Mary Cooke, Ontario, Canada

BROWN SCONES
Mary Cooke, Ontario

1 ½ lb whole wheat meal
1 oz butter
1 cup caster sugar
pinch of salt
2 full tsp baking powder
Milk

Mix all dry ingredients and rub in butter; mix into light dough with sweet milk; divide into two round cakes; cut each into four; bake in moderate oven.

CURRANT TEA SCONES
Mary Cooke, Ontario

1 lb flour
3 oz caster sugar
3 oz butter
1 ½ oz candied lemon peel
3 oz currants
a little milk
2 tsp baking powder
1 tsp cream of tartar
1 egg

Mix all dry ingredients well together; rub in butter; beat egg and add half; add milk and mix into stiff dough; divide into two, cut each into four, brush over with rest of egg; put at once into quick oven; bake 15 to 20 minutes.

GREAT GRANDDAD'S SCONES
Stephen Kline, Yorkshire

"My great granddad had a butcher's and bakehouse in Wakefield, a hundred years ago, and I have "inherited" his recipes. Translated into current ingredients, this recipe makes exceptional scones. If you really want to be naughty you can slice the still warm scones horizontally and spread with home made strawberry jam and fresh cream! Only allow yourself 1 a day to avoid heart attack or obesity, or both."

For a large tray, about a dozen scones use the following ingredients:

4 oz butter
16 oz self-raising flour
½ tsp salt
up to ½ pint milk
2 medium eggs, beaten
6 oz caster sugar
4 oz fruit (e.g., currants, sultanas)
(I use a mixture of chopped dates and mixed peel)

Rub far/flour/sugar together as you would for pastry and when "crumbed" add other ingredients, but slowly, add milk to mix (by hand, not machine). It may not need all the milk, depending on the size of the eggs. You need a consistency which will roll with the rolling pin on a floured board.

When rolled to a thickness of 1 in, cut (with round pastry cutter or cup, in two sizes). Place larger size on flat/floured tray (a toffee-making tray is ideal), brush with milk and add smaller size on top and brush again with milk (or beaten egg).

Bake in a fairly hot oven (425°F) until cooked all the way through.

GRIDDLE SCONES
Mary Cooke, Ontario

½ lb flour
2 oz butte
2 oz sugar
½ tsp baking powder
¾ tsp bicarbonate of soda
1 egg
¼ tsp tartaric acid
1 teacupful milk

Mix the bicarbonate of soda, tartaric acid and baking powder wit the flour and rub butter lightly in. Beat egg with sugar and add milk. Mix with dry ingredients to form a soft dough.

Divide into 3 pieces, roll each piece out into a round scone, put on a hot griddle; bake 5 minutes over clear fire.

PLAIN SCONE
Dell Maw, Queensland, Australia

3 cups (12 oz) flour
1 tsp salt
1 cup mil soured with ½ tsp lemon Juice
2 oz butter

Sift flour and salt into bowl. Rub in butter Make a well in centre and ix in milk, adding more if necessary to make a soft dough.

Knead lightly and roll out on a lightly-floured surface to ¾ in thickness. Cut in rounds with a 1½ in floured cutter.

Place on lightly-greased oven sheet. Bake in a very hot oven (450°F) for 10-15 min.

TEA SCONES
Mary Cooke, Ontario

1 lb flour
3 oz caster sugar
1 oz butter
1 tsp cream of tartar
½ tsp bicarbonate of soda
Buttermilk

Rub butter into flour; mix dry ingredients, mix and add buttermilk; grease cake tin and pour in mixture; bake in moderate oven for 45 minutes.

BREAD

FLAT BREAD
Marge Cambridge, Mission, B.C.

"I'm a *Canuck* but my Yorkshire mom always buttered bread no matter what else went on it. One other of my favourites was what she called 'flat bread' – bread dough rolled out thin, risen for a few minutes, pricked, then tossed on the bottom of a hot oven, given a few minutes then turned over. (After the bottom of the oven had been cleaned with waxed paper – not an electric stove either.) We would tear off a piece, split it, and butter it. I was like two yummy crusts."

LOYS' EUROPEAN BREAD
Loys Fawcett, Canada

"My grandmother had a wonderful bread recipe that did originate in Europe. We are in Canada and the recipe made it safely across and it is an excellent tasting bread."

- In a large bowl put 20 to 24 cups of white, all-purpose flour. In a separate bowl mix 2 cups of sugar and 2 tablespoons of salt with 2 cups of vegetable oil. Beat in 2 eggs and 8 cups of warm water.

- Make up a yeast solution of 2 packages of yeast (2 tablespoons), ½ cup warm water and 4 teaspoons of sugar. Let the yeast solution stand for 10 minutes and then add to the sugar, salt, oil, eggs and water. Gradually add the flour until all is mixed thoroughly.

Kneed well. Place in a greased bowl, cover (set in a warm room with no drafts), and let rise for 2 hours.

- Punch and let rise for 1 hour. Make into small loaves until all the flour is used or you have no loaf pans left. The rest can be made into small rolls in a muffin pan.

Leave to rise overnight, covered and in a warm room.

- Bake the rolls for 20 minutes and the small loaves for 1 ½ hours or until the tops are just browning. The oven temperature should be at 400°F for the rolls and 300°F for the bread. Make sure you don't try to make large rolls or the dough won't cook through and stay light and fluffy.

MALT BREAD
Christina Flanigan, California

1 lb self-rising flour
½ pint milk
2 level tsp bicarbonate of soda
2 eggs
4 level Tbsp golden syrup
2 teacups sultanas or raisins
4 level Tbsp malt extract

Sift flour and soda in a bowl. Melt syrup and malt in a pan with the milk, add beaten eggs and add to flour. Add fruit. Pour into greased tins and bake 375-400°F. Makes 2 medium loaves.

MOTHER'S BREAD
Pam Dallia Rasmussen, Wisconsin
Great-granddaughter of Elizabeth Ann Broadbent Deiters, b. 1872, who gave this recipe to her daughter, Anna Deiters Beigel

1 quart milk
1 Tbsp salt
12 cups flour
2 *pills* each butter and margarine
2 level Tbsp sugar
2 eggs
2 large yeast
Add one cup flour then eggs. 15 min high-low
5 loaves

"That was exactly how Elizabeth wrote the recipe down. Upon a lot of research, I found *pills of butter* to be about the size of a tablespoon. I had to 'play-around' with the recipe until I came up with the following:

Scald milk. Cool to lukewarm. Add yeast while still warm enough to activate it.

Add butter, salt and sugar. Add one cup of flour. Mix well. Add eggs. Mix well.

Add remaining flour by cupful until dough can be handled easily (not sticky). Knead on floured board about 3-5 min. Turn it greased bowl and let rise until doubled.

Bake about 20-25 min in 425°F oven. Turn out on wire rack after slightly cooled if you want a nice crust on sides and bottom.

(If you cool bread in the pans, the crust tends to break up when you slice it.)"

NORTH RIDING BREAD
Christina Flanigan, California

1 lb plain flour
6 oz currants
¼ tsp salt
6 oz raisins
4 tsp baking powder
3 ox mixed chopped peel
¼ tsp nutmeg
1 Tbsp treacle
3-4 oz lard
½ tsp almond essence
6 oz demerara sugar
½ pint milk

Sift flour, salt, baking powder and nutmeg. Rub in lard, add sugar and fruit.

Stir in the treacle, almost essence and milk and mix all to form a soft dough.

Divide into two small (½ lb size) bread or cake tins and bake in a fairly hot oven (375-400°F).

WALNUT BREAD
Susan Cook, Westbank, B.C.

1 lb self-raisin flour
4 oz finely chopped walnuts
1 tsp salt
3 oz raisins
1 oz lard
½ pint milk
3 oz sugar

Grease loaf or bread pan. Mix flour and salt and rub in lard. Add walnuts, raisins and sugar and mix. Beat the egg with the milk and mix into flour mixture thoroughly.

Bake in a 375°F oven for 1 hour.

VINEGAR LOAF
James Barlow, Rothwell, Leeds

1 lb flour
½ lb sugar
6 oz butter or margarine
½ lb raisins
1 oz candied peel chopped
½ lb currants
1½ cups milk
Small wineglass of vinegar
½ tsp bicarbonate of soda
½ tsp allspice
1 tsp nutmeg

Rub margarine into flour and add sugar; fruit and spices. Sprinkle bicarbonate into mixture, mix with milk, add vinegar last of all.

Put into tins and bake at Gas Mark 2 for 1½ hours.

ON YORKSHIRE

"She is the mother of children who have loved her with a passionate regard".

William Smith, 1881

YORK MAYNE BREAD
Susan Cook, Westbank, B.C.
(From "Through Yorkshire's Kitchen Door", Yorkshire Federation of Women's Institutes.)

12 oz plain flour
8 oz sugar
3 egg yolks
2 egg whites
Heaping tsp coriander seed
Heaping tsp carraway seed
½ oz yeast
2 tsp rosewater
1/3 cup warm milk and water

Mix together the flour, sugar, coriander and carraway seeds. Add to the 3 yolks and the rose water in one basin. In another basin, beat 2 whites of eggs until stiff, In a third basin, put the yeast, warm milk and water.

The whole of the contents of these three basis to be then mixed with the dry ingredients and put to rise in a warm place for approximately 20 min.

After which, roll out, cut into shape and allow to rise in a warm place again for 10 min.

Bake in a moderate oven for 10-15 min or until golden brown.

ON YORKIES

"A more stiff-necked, wilful or obstinate people did I never know or hear of".

Archbishop of York, 1575

HISTORICAL NOTE
YORK MAYNE BREAD

"There are many records that state that Mayne bread was presented to distinguished strangers to York from 1445 to 1662, but its history had been stormy throughout these 200 years and possibly before that as well. In Queen Elizabeth I's reign, a serious rival to Mayne bread had become popular under the name of Spiced Cake.

In 1595, the following minute was passed by the City Corporation: "Whereas the baking of Mayne Bread in this city is of late almost left off, or lean give over; which is thought to be by reason the spyced cakes are of late, grown into greater use than heretofore baked in any other City or place for of the City in England and hath been used in this City time out of mind of man, and is one of the antientest matters of novelty to present men of honour and others repairing to this City, with all that can be had here; therefore it is thought convenient that the same be still continued and kept in use and not be suffered to decay nor be laid down. And it is agreed that the Mayne bakers of this City shall almost them bake every Friday morning ten shillings worth of Mayne bread at the least, to be sold to such as will buy it, and if it do not sell before 5 o'clock in the afternoon, the bakers shall send it to the Lord Mayor and each Alderman, four pennyworth, and to the Sheriffs and twenty-four each two penny worth, or as much as shall remain unsold and they to take and pay the same.

Despite these and other regulations, spiced cakes became increasingly popular even under the threat of an order in 1607 that prohibited spice cakes under a penalty of 40/s, for each offense. In 1622, the City Corporation reluctantly acknowledged that the days of Mayne Bread were over. Sometime between this date and 1950, the recipe for Mayne Bread was lost, but in 1950 a great deal of research was done in an effort to trace out this ancient history and to find the recipe itself. Eventually a recipe was found in an old MSS by Major A.G. Wade of Hampshire, and it is this recipe which is given herein. There is no doubt that this recipe is the old one that was used in the Middle Ages, and samples of bread made from this recipe were given to guests during the 1951 York Festival."

In Through Yorkshire's Kitchen Door
Ed. The Yorkshire Federation of Women's Institutes, 1957.

BREAKFAST

MILK PORRIDGE
Joan Hudson

"Is anyone outside my family familiar wit this? I know the recipe came from Lofthouse in Nidderdale with my grandparents, over a hundred years ago, and it still makes a weekly appearance on our menu, especially if we are ailing or need comfort food. The method is simple.

Bring a bowl of milk almost to the boil, add about 4 tablespoons of Scotch oatmeal; then either serve as lumpy or stir it about a little to make a sort of gruel."

SERVING SUGGESTIONS FOR PORRIDGE

Porridge is equally good served with a light pouring of cold milk, cream, a sprinkling of sugar or even a dollop of jam!

BRAWN

In Victorian times, brawn was often served at breakfast. As today this dish is more appropriate to a light meal, several recipes for brawn are given under "Savouries".

NOTES

ASSORTED BREWS

BISHOP
Beverley Ramsden, Renfrew, Ontario

1 large orange
12 cloves
1 bottle of Port
Sugar

Stick cloves into orange, put into fireproof/ovenproof bowl, cover closely and roast until a rich brown colour. Cut into 8 pieces, remove pips.

Put Port into saucepan with pieces of orange and heat gently. Sweeten to taste with sugar and simmer 20 min, but be careful not to let it boil.

Strain off liquid through fine sieve and serve at once – hot.

BISHOP'S NIGHTCAP
Beverley Ramsden, Renfrew Ontario

1 large orange
12 cloves
½ tsp mace
½ tsp ground ginger
½ tsp ground cinnamon
½ tap allspice
½ tsp powdered cloves
1 lemon, rind thinly peeled, juice
½ pint water
¼ lb sugar
1 bottle Port

Stick cloves into orange, put into fireproof/ovenproof bowl, cover closely and roast until a rich brown colour.
Put spices and lemon peel into enamel saucepan containing the water and bring to boil. Simmer gently ½ hour.

Strain off liquid through fine sieve and stir in lemon juice and sugar. Add roasted orange and Port, heat up again but do not allow to boil. Serve hot.

BOOKKHAM CREAM
Beverley Ramsden, Renfrew Ontario

1 large teacup of cream
2 glasses of Sherry
Grated peel and juice of 1 lemon
4 oz sugar
Whip until thick and pour into glasses piled up high.
Leave to stand for 4 or 5 days!

EGGNOG
Magdalena Gorrell Guimaraens
Northern Portugal

"My mother cut this recipe out of an ad in 1940 and it has been served ever since in our home, both at Christmas and New Year's. Makes about 5 pints.

6 eggs
¾ cup granulated sugar
1 pint cream
1 pint milk
1 oz dark Jamaica Rum
1 pint Bourbon Whisky
Grated nutmeg

Beat yolks and whites of eggs separately. Add ½ cup sugar to egg yolks while beating them. Add ¼ cup sugar to whites after they have been beaten very stiff.

In a punch bowl, fold in egg yolks and whites together. Stir in cream and milk, little by little. Add Bourbon and Rum. Stir thoroughly. Serve very cold, with a sprinkling of nutmeg.

HOT PUNCH

1 large lemon
2-3 oz/ ¼ cup sugar
pinch of ground cinnamon
pinch of ground nutmeg
pinch of ground cloves
½ pint of Brandy
½ pint of Rum
1 pint boiling water

Remove rind of lemon by rubbing with some sugar. Put all the sugar, spices, Brandy and Rum and boiling water into a pan, heat gently on low-medium heat but do not boil.

Strain lemon juice into punch bowl, add hot liquid and serve at once.

HOT PUNCH TEA

Tea
1/3 cup sugar
2 in cinnamon stick or ground
1 cup grated lemon rind
1 cup grated orange rind
1 cup orange juice
1 cup pineapple juice
1 cup Barbados Rum

Make enough tea for 6 people and let it stand.

Put in saucepan ½ cup water, rinds and cinnamon, and boil 5 min. Remove cinnamon stick if used, add juices and ground cinnamon.

Strain hot tea into fruit mixture. Add Rum. Serve hot.

LOVING CUP

¼ lb sugar
2 lemons
Few spring lemon balm
2-3 sprigs borage
1½ pints water
½ bottle Madeira wine
¼ pint French Brandy
1 bottle Champagne

Rub peel off 1 lemon with some lumps of sugar. Remove every particle of pith, also the rind and pith of the other lemon, slice them thinly.

Put the balm, borage, sliced lemons and all the sugar into a jug, add the water, Madeira and Brandy. Cover and chill for one hour. Chill the Champagne, add and serve.

NEGUS

3 oz sugar
1 lemon
1 pint Port
1 pint boiling water
¼ small nutmeg
2-3 drops vanilla extract

Rub sugar on rind of lemon util all zest is extracted. Crush in basin ad pour Port and boiling water over it. Add nutmeg and vanilla. Serve hot.

POPE'S POSSET

4 oz sweet almonds
3 oz bitter almonds
½ pint cold water
½ bottle white wine
Sugar to taste

Blanch and pound almonds. Put into enamel pan with water and bring gently to the boil. Strain liquid, stir in the white wine and add sugar. Return to boiling point. Serve at once – hot.

PINK PORT SUMMER COCKTAIL
Magdalena Gorrell Guimaraens

Fill a long drink glass halfway with finely chopped ice. Top up with a good measure of Rosé Port Wine. Garnish with a slice of watermelon, orange or lemon, to taste.

PORT WINE AND TONIC COCKTAIL
Magdalena Gorrell Guimaraens

In a long drink glass, place a good measure of dry white Port. Top up with chilled tonic water. Garnish with a slice of lemon.

RUM TODDY

1 lump sugar
1 ½ oz (1 jigger) of Rum
Boiling water
Slice of lemon
2 cloves

Put sugar and Rum in tumbler with boiling water. (Don't use your best crystal, use a thick glass to avoid breakage.) Add slice of lemon and the cloves.

SLOE GIN
Roger Walker

"I don't know if this is particularly a Yorkshire thing, probably not, but my mother always made it and then she told me how to make it and I've done so for the past couple of years.

Where I live the farmers have gone round and cut all the hedgerows. The sloes, the berries of the blackberry bush, grow in abundance around the edge of my 5 acre field and I usually pick them in October. I like t print out a fancy label on the computer for the bottle and put it away until the following winter. Then for this winter, I'll open the one I made last year. I believe you can do the same with plums and damsons but I've not tried them. Would make a nice present for a granny – I'm sure she'd appreciate it."

I lb sloe berries
4 oz sugar
1 bottle of Gin

Wash the berries and clean off any old leaf bits, prick every berry and place them in a glass jar that has a good fitting lid and will hold the contents of the gin bottle and then some.

Add the sugar and the gin, fit the lid and give it a good shaking. Put the jar aside until the next day. After 24 hours give it another good shaking and then every day after that for the next 2 weeks, inverting the jar to mix the contents.

Then leave for about 6 weeks inverting the jar occasionally. The resulting liquor should be a nice rich plum colour.

After another 6 weeks drain the jar through a sieve into a clean jug then filter the liquid through a paper coffee filter. The result will be a crystal clear, plum coloured liquid. Pour this back into the original gin bottle.

IMPORTANT NOTE

Be extremely careful when heating alcoholic liquids
Do not leave even for a second on the stove, they can ignite without the aid of a match if hot enough.

NOTES

BEER

COUNTRY STOUT
Ann Scott, Bingley, West Yorkshire

450 gr (1 lb) black malt
50 gr (2 oz) hops
450 gr (1 lb) granulated sugar
25 gr (1 oz) yeast
4-5 litres (1 gal) water

Put water, malt and hops (tied in a muslin bag) int a large saucepan, baring to the boil and boil for 20 min.

Remove from heat and left out hops, then add sugar and stir until dissolved. Let it cool and when just tepid add the yeast.

Let it work overnight covered with a cloth and bottle next day. It can be drunk 2 days later, but it is better left a little longer (if you can!).

GAYLE BEER
Anne Garrison, ex-Harrogate now Reading, Berkshire

"Gale is a type of Bog Myrtle that has aromatic leaves. Our family drank it immediately but I think it should be left for a while to ferment a little more."

Plenty of gale leaves – a big handful
1 gallon boiling water
1 lb sugar
1 oz yeast or 1 Tbsp dried yeast
1 lemon sliced
1 slice of toast

Put the leaves, sugar and lemon in a bowl, pour on the boiling water. Allow to cool. When the mixture is tepid float a piece of toast on the surface and place the yeast on it.

Leave for 24 hours, remove the toast, strain and bottle in corked bottles. Look out for popping corks!

GINGER BEER
Ann Scott, Bingley, West Yorkshire

Mix together 8½ litres (2 gals) boiling water with 50g (2 oz) well-bruised ginger root, 2 sliced lemons, 2 tsp cream of tartar and 900 gr (2 lb) sugar.

Stir well until all the sugar is dissolved and when cold dd 25 gr (1 oz) fresh yeast spread on a piece of toast.

Let it work (covered) for 24 hours, then strain and bottle.

MILD COUNTRY ALE
Ann Scott, Bingley, West Yorkshire

Traditional recipe over 100 years old, from an early Halifax naturalist.

25 gr (1 oz) hops (available from health shops
4-5 litres (1 gal) water
225 gr (½ lb) sugar
1 Tbsp yeast

Boil the hops and water for 30 minutes Strain this liquor on to the sugar and when it is lukewarm add the yeast.

Let it work for 4 full days, then bottle and use in a week or a fortnight.

MULLED ALE
Ann Scott, Bingley, West Yorkshire

1 quart ale
1 Tbsp sugar
pinch ground cloves
pinch ground nutmeg
Good pinch ground ginger

1 glass Rum or Brandy

Put all ingredients except Brandy into a saucepan, bring nearly to boil. Add Brandy and more sugar and flavouring if necessary. Serve at once.

"Yorkshire born and Yorkshire bred,
Strong int arm und strong int 'ead"

NOTES

WINES

CHAMPAGNE AND BRANDY PUNCH
Magdalena Gorrell Guimaraens
Northern Portugal

This is a sure-fire ice-breaker and although apparently weak, it packs a punch!

1 bottle dry white Sparkling Wine
2 cups Brandy
4-8 sugar cubes

In a punch bowl, place the sugar cubes and pour over the Brandy. Wait about 1 hour. Add the chilled sparking wine, stir and serve.

CHAMPAGNE CUP

1 bottle Champagne
2 bottles soda water
Few strips lemon rind
½ tsp Maraschino cherry juice
1 liqueur glass Brandy
1 tsp sugar (optional)

Chill Champagne and soda water for 1 hour. When ready to sere, put strips of lemon rind in large glass jug, add Maraschino juice and Brandy, pour in Champagne and soda water.

Serve at once. If sugar is added, it should be stirred in gradually.

ELDERFLOWER CHAMPAGNE (1)
Anne Garrison, ex-Harrogate
now Reading, Berkshire

"My recipes are family ones and my family came from Yorkshire. I grew up there. We made elderflower champagne, elderflower cordial and gayle beer. I still make Elderflower cordial (every year) and gayle beer (sometimes). Our family was Methodist, so the elderflower champagne was not alcoholic – the gayle beer was supposed to be consumed before it fermented but as teenagers we used to try to keep it until it started to ferment!"

2 large heads of elderflower
1 lb sugar (some recipes say 1lb8oz)
Juice and rind of a lemon
2 Tbsp white vinegar
1 gal cold water

Leave for 24 hours and bottle. Cork tightly – it will be ready to drink in about a fortnight.

"Make sure you have enough bottles to put it in. It is better to use glass bottles with corks rather than screw tops. Pressure can build up so store the bottles somewhere where it won't matter if the tops fly off."

ELDERFLOWER CHAMPAGNE (2)
Gillian Nixon, Barnsley

4 elderflower heads
2 lemons
1½ lb sugar
2 Tbsp white wine
1 gal cold water

Put all ingredients except lemons in a large bowl. Squeeze lemons into bowl, quarter and add, stand 24 hours, stirring occasionally. Strain and bottle into screw top bottles.

ELDERFLOWER CORDIAL
*Anne Garrison, ex-Harrogate
now Reading, Berkshire*
Use to flavour Gooseberry dishes

20 Elderflower heads
2 kgs (4 lbs) sugar
80 gr (2¾ oz) citric acid
2 lemons grated and sliced
1.2 litres (2 pints) boiling water

Shake elderflower heads free of insects. Stir sugar into boiling water. Add citric acid, grated rind of lemon and sliced lemons.

Pour into a bowl, add the elderflower heads and leave overnight covered with cling film.

Sieve out the flowers, pour the syrup through a jelly bag to clarify and bottle.

Dilute one part of the syrup with 8 parts of sparkling water or mixed Gin and soda water.

"I don't bother with the jelly bag, I put it through a coffee paper filter in a funnel."

BLACK OR WHITE ELDERBERRY WINE
Judith Lyon, Cronulla, NSW, Australia

"Gather the berries ripe and dry, prick them, bruise with your hands and strain them.

Set the liquor by in glazed earthenware vessels for twelve hours, to settle. Put to every pint of juice a pint and a half of water; and to every gallon of the liquor, three pounds of good moist sugar.

Set in a kettle over the fire, and when it is ready to boil, clarify it with the white of four or five eggs.

Let it boil one hour and when it is almost cold, work it with strong ale yeast, and turn it, filling up the vessel from time to time with the same liquor, saved on purpose, as it sinks by working.

In a month's time, if the vessel holds about eight gallons, it will be fine and fit to bottle, and after bottling, will be fit to drink in twelve months."

MULLED WINE
*Magdalena Gorrell Guimaraens
Northern Portugal*

1 bottle ordinary red table wine
1 cup granulated sugar
2 cups pineapple or other fruit juice
2 sticks cinnamon
6 cloves

Mix juice, sugar and spices and heat on a slow burner until just boiling. Turn off the heat, add the red wine, stir and serve.

POTATO WINE
Ann Scott, Bingley, West Yorkshire

"Some wanted a recipe for potato wine – here it is from the 1900 Cookbook – courtesy of the Women in Yorkshire."

Wash well but do not peel, ½ gals small potatoes. Put them into a pan with 1 gal water. Bring to a boil for 5 mn. Have ready a stone jar or bowl.

Put into the jar 3 lbs demerara sugar, the rind of 2 sliced lemons.

Strain over this through a sieve the boiled liquor from the potatoes, stir the dissolved sugar, and return to the pan.

A piece of bruised ginger may be added if liked

Boil for ½ hour then strain into bowl and when cold, bottle, add about a couple of raisins to each bottle. Cork lightly.

This wine is delicious if kept over 12 months.

TURNIP WINE
Judith Lyon, Cronulla, NSW, Australia

Take a large number of turnips, pare and slice them; then place in a cider-press and obtain all the juice you can.

To every gallon of juice, add three pounds of lump sugar and half a pint of Brandy. Pour the liquor into a cask and when it has done working, bung it close for three months then draw off into another cask. When it is fine, bottle and cork well.

YORKSHIRE BEETROOT WINE
Mrs. Terry, Barnsley

5 lb beetroot
3½ lbs demerara sugar
1½ gals water
½ oz yeast
1 slice toast
½ tsp ginger

Wash and slice beetroot, add water and bring to boil and simmer for one hour. Add sugar and simmer for 20 min, allow to cool.

Strain (add ginger), place yeast on slice of toast and put on top of wine.

Stand for 10 days, strain and bottle

NOTES

CAKES AND PASTRIES

APPLE CAKE FOR RIPON'S WILFA WEEK
Susan Cook, Westbank, B.C.

Sir Wilfred of Ripon, to whom the lovely cathedral is dedicated, is remembered each year especially during Wilfa Week, which beings on August Bank Holiday.

Line a long sandwich tin with shortcrust pastry. Peel and slice some apples thinly and line the tin until the pastry is covered to a depth of at least ¾ in. Cover with sugar or golden syrup, add a sprinkling of grated cheese, then cover with pastry and bake in a moderate oven.

"Apple cake without cheese is like a kiss without a squeeze."

APPLE CHARLOTTE
Claire Schofield, Flockton, Wakefield

"My Granny unfortunately passed away when I was 16, however I have many happy memories of visiting her... one of which was her lovely Apple Charlotte, Sometimes she used to do a vit of a special one for birthdays and other occasions, and add a glass of brandy to the apple mix!"

Take 2 lbs cooking apples, stewed until almost a smooth applesauce with 2 Tbsp caster sugar and 1 Tbsp honey.
When ready, place into an ovenproof pudding dish, making sure to leave 3-4 in between the apple mixture and the top of the container.

Make a basic mixture of Victoria sponge. (See recipe further ahead.)
When the apple mix has cooled sufficiently, pour the sponge mixture over the top. Bake at 350°F until the sponge mixture is brown and crisp to the touch. Serve with thick, homemade custard.

BANOFEE PIE
Sandee Hughes

2 14 oz cans sweet condensed milk
10 oz Graham cracker crumbs
5 oz butter, softened
4 medium bananas
1 cup heavy whipping cream
2 Tbsp confectioner's sugar
½ tsp vanilla

Mix cracker crumbs with softened butter and press into large pie tin. Place crust in refrigerator until filling is ready.
Boil the two cans of mil, unopened, in a pan of water for 1 ½ hours. The milk remains in the cans unopened and must be submerged in the pot of boiling water. If the water boils down to expose the cans, refill the pot. This caramelizes the milk in the can. The cans may be stored for several weeks. Allow to cool to room temperature.
Slice bananas and layer in the pie pan. Spoon caramelized milk over the fruit. Whip the cream with the sugar and vanilla and spread on top of the caramelized milk.

BURY SIMNEL
Mary Cooke, Ontario

3 lbs flour
1 lb currents
½ lb sugar
6 oz sweet almonds
3 large or 4 small eggs
1 lb butter
¾ lb sultanas
6 oz candied peel, finely chopped
6 oz fresh yeast
½ oz mixed spice

Rub butter in flour. Add dry ingredients and mix thoroughly. Mix yeast with a dessertspoonful of sugar till it creams and add a little warm water to yeast.

Beat eggs thoroughly and add to dry mixture. Add yeast and mix whole with sufficient warm water to make a very stiff paste. Cover with cloth and stand 1½ hr.

Form into large buns and place on greased baking tin. Stand for 30 min then bake in moderate oven for one hour.

CURD CHEESECAKE
June Ridsdale, Maple Ridge, B.C.

PASTRY
12 oz of plain flour
6 oz of lard
cold water to mix

Make pastry and line 6 curd tins (about 14cms/5-6 in diameter).

CURD FILLING
8 oz curd
8 oz sugar
4 oz melted butter or margarine
2 or 3 eggs
2 oz currants
scraping of nutmeg

Mix all filling ingredients together. Put filling into prepared tins. Bake in the centre of the oven at about 350-400°F until brown and set.

CURD TART
Mrs. J. Smith, Halifax

150g short pastry
Line an 18cm tin or 18 patty tins with pastry.

FILLING
200g curd cheese (or cottage cheese)
50g sugar
50g currants
1 egg
40g melted margarine
pinch of cinnamon and nutmeg

Mix the filing together and pop into pastry case(s). Bake in a hot oven for 15-20 min.

ELSIE'S FRUITCAKE
Ann Collier, Wentworth

1¼ lb flour
1 large tsp baking powder
1 lb sugar
½ lb lard
6 eggs
½ butter
1 gill (½ cup)milk
1 lb fruit

Bake 1½ hours in a medium oven.

ESKIMO PIE
Susan Cook, Westbank, B.C.

½ lb marshmallows melted with ½ cup mil in double boiler. Whip ½ pint whipping cream. Stir and mix with marshmallows. Put on biscuit base or crushed biscuits. Freeze.

Thaw for ½ hour at room temperature before serving.

FAT RASCALS or TURF CAKES
Susan Cook, Westbank, B.C.

Called turf cakes on Whitby Moors where they were cooked over an open turf or peat fire on a griddle.

8 oz self-raising flour
4 oz lard
3 oz sugar
2 oz currents
1 oz sultanas
pinch of salt
water or beaten egg

Rub the lard into the flour and add other ingredients. Mix to a fairly soft dough with a little water (or to make them extra rich, use a little well-beaten egg).

Roll out to about ½ in thick and cut into rounds.

Bake in a hot over (425ºF) for about 15 min or until brown. Makes about 24.

GREAT-GRANNY'S CAKE
Originally Isabella Hardaker's (Ackworth) recipe, as handed down to her daughter Kathleen Allott (Rotherham) then to her daughter-in-law Magdalena Gorrell Guimaraens

3 cups flour
½ oz yeast
2 cups sugar
2 oz ground almonds
1 cup warm milk
¼ lb butter

2 cups fruit. Mix together and let rise 1 hour in tins. Bake for 2 hours over a tin of water, gently.

LARDY or FATTY CAKE (1)
Marge Cambridge, Mission, B.C

1 lb flour
3 oz sugar
4 oz fat
½ pint warm milk
1 oz yeast
3 tsp mixed spices
1 tsp salt
3-6 oz dried fruit (if desired)

Warm flour and salt lightly and rub in 1 oz fat. Cream yeast with 1 tsp sugar and add mil.

Mix flour and yeast mixture and mix until it forms a soft dough. Put in a greased bowl, cover and et to rise in a warm place for 1 hour

Flake remaining fat. Sprinkle 1/3 each of the fat, sugar, spice and fruit over the dough. Fold over as for flaky pastry. Roll, repeat twice.

Leave to rise for 20 mn. Brush with beaten egg. Bake in a hot over for 20-30 min, reducing heat halfway.

LARDY CAKE (2)
Janice Wood

DOUGH
15g fresh yeast or 2 x 5ml spoons dried yeast
1 x 5ml spoons sugar
275 ml tepid water
5 ml salt
450g flour

FILLING
100g lard
100g sugar
100g currants
mixed spire as required

GLAZE
6 ml water
20g sugar

Cream yeast with sugar, add tepid water and a bi of flour. Blend dried yeast with sugar and a little liquid. Let it stand until soft. Mix to cream and add rest of liquid.

Put in a warm place until bubbly, then add it to the flour and salt. Knead very well, cover, and leave in a warm place until it has doubled in size. Knead again until smooth, roll out to an oblong.

Cut lard into small pieces and put half onto two thirds of the dough, sprinkle with half of the sugar, fruit and spice and fold in three – uncovered piece first. Half turn and repeat the lard, sugar, fruit and spice and fold into three again.

Turn, roll, fold, turn and roll, fold, roll and place in a warm tin. Score the top. Cover and prove in a warm place until double in size again.

Bake in a hot oven at 220ºC for 45 min but lower the heat after 20 min. Glaze. Serve cold.

LEMON CHEESECAKE
Pauline Hinson

"I couldn't find a curd cheesecake recipe in Mrs. Beeton's (gasp!), not in a variety of other British cookery books I've got, however, I did find a vegetarian version – no gelatine. Y'all know that gelatine comes from the boiled bones of dead animals, don-t you? You might try adding some agar-agar according to the packet directions, because otherwise you have to keep this thing WELL chilled and handle very carefully or you end up with collapsed cheesecake. Not a pretty sight Recipes like this are why I was the recipient of the remark, "Oh, you're vegetarian! Really? I thought vegetarians were THIN". These are US measurements. Americans use an 8 oz cup for measuring liquid AND dry ingredients. Spoons are 1/3 smaller. Have fun comparing."

8 oz wholemeal flour/Graham Crackers
4 Tbsp melted butter

FILLING
2 lemons
2/3 cup sugar
1½ cup cream cheese
1½ cup curd/ricotta cheese
½ cup heavy cream
curls of lemon peel/rind
whipped cream to decorate

Finely crush biscuits/crackers, stir into melted butter. Press mixture into base of 8" springform cake pan.

Grate rind from lemons, saving a few curls for decorating; squeeze out juice. Place in bowl with sugar. Beat well. Slowly beat in cheeses and continue beating until smooth.

Whip cream well until it holds its shape and fold in cheese. Spread cheese mixture over base and level surface. Cover and refrigerate several hours.

Turn cheesecake out on to serving plate. Decorate with whipped cream and lemon curls.

MAIDS OF HONOUR (1)
Barbara McLean, Murrieta, California

These tarts date back to when Henry VIII chanced upon maids of honour eating some. He tried one and like it so the name stuck.

1 1/3 cup baker's cheese
6 Tbsp softened butter
2 eggs
1 Tbsp Brandy

1 Tbsp superfine sugar
¼ cup ground almonds
pinch ground nutmeg
a few flaked almonds
8 oz frozen puff pastry, defrosted

Roll pastry out on a lightly floured board and line 12 lightly greased muffin tins.
 Mix the remaining ingredients except the flaked almonds and spoon into the pastry cases.
 Sprinkle flaked almonds on each and bake at 425°F for 15-20 min until the pastry is golden brown and the filling is set.

MAIDS OF HONOUR (2)
Martyn Gleadon, Wath-upon-Dearne

"My mother gave me my grandmother's old Be-RO cookbook when I went to University in the vain hope that I would feed myself on good, wholesome, homemade food."

Half the quantity of short pastry and half the recipe quantity of sandwich cake mix.
 Roll the pastry out thinly and cut into rounds with a scone cutter.
Line 14 pastry tins with the pastry, put a little jam in each, then a spoonful of the sandwich cake mixture.
 Bake in a hot oven (425-450°F) for about 20 min.

SHORT PASTRY

½ tsp salt
1 oz sugar
2 oz lard
2 oz margarine
About 8 tsp cold water

Mix flour and salt in basin.
Rub in lard and margarine lightly until the bread crumbs.

Stir in sugar and, using a knife, mix with cold water to form a stiff dough.

SANDWICH CAKE MIXTURE
4 oz self-raising flour
2 oz sugar
2 oz margarine
1 egg beaten with 2 Tbsp milk

Beat margarine an sugar into a cream in a warm, not hot, basin.
Stir flour and beaten egg alternately, a little at a time, and mix thoroughly. The mixture should be soft.

MAIDS OF HONOUR (3)
Jean Spence, Adelaide, Australia

"I hang onto my old Be-RO cookbook – simple, tasty, economical, nothing fancy, the essence of Yorkshire. These tarts taste even better if iced with a small cherry on top."

6 OZ SHORT PASTRY
(I make mine with a quantity of marge and double the quantity of flour mixed with water and a pinch of salt.)

FILLING
Jam
2 oz margarine
2 oz caster sugar
2 oz self-raising flour
1 egg

Roll out pastry, cut into 18 rounds and line patty tins. Place a little jam in each case.
 Cream margarine and sugar, fold in beaten egg and flour. Place a teaspoon of filling in each case.
 Bake in a moderate oven (3p75-400°F, Gas Mark 5-8) about 20 min.

QUEEN CAKES
Susan Cook, Westbank, B.C.

2 cups flour
4 eggs
1 cup butter
6 oz currants
1 cup demerara sugar
1 tsp baking powder

Beat butter an sugar to a cream and add eggs, one at a time, and beat well.

Add flour and baking powder and mix well. Add currants and mix. Place in greased cupcake tins and bake at 375°F for 25-30 min.

SAD CAKES
Susan Cook, Westbank, B.C.

1 lb plain flour
8 oz bacon fat or lard
salt and cold water

Rub fat into flour and salt and mix to pastry consistency with cold water. Bake in a greased sandwich tin, as for short crust pastry.

SUET CRUST PASTRY
Tricia Backhouse, Huntsville, Ontario

8 oz (225g) self-raising flour
4 oz (110g) shredded suet
salt and pepper for savoury crusts
cold water to mix

Sift the flour into a bowl, then sprinkle the suet in, season with salt and pepper if you want a savoury crust, and just mix it lightly with your hands to distribute it evenly. Now sprinkle some cold water. Begin mixing with a round-bladed knife and then continue mixing with your hands to make a smooth elastic dough that leaves the bowl clean.

Wait 5 min and then roll out immediately to about ½ in thick. Enough for an 8" pie dish. For a larger pie dish, use 12oz (350g) flour and 6 oz (175g) sugar.

YORKSHIRE CURD TART
Conrad Plowman, Knaresborough

"I know you have several recipes for Yorkshire curd tart, but you may like to have this one for several reasons:
1. It is at least 250 years old.
2. The recipe is fairly unique in using rosewater.
3. The pastry is also at least 100 years old.
4. It describes how to make the curd.
5. It was shown on the BBC in a feature on Yorkshire curd tart. Oct. 1999.

PASTRY
4 oz (120g) plain flour
1 oz (30g) icing sugar
2 oz (60g) butter
½ beaten egg

Mix flour and sugar and rub in butter. Add beaten egg an mix.

CURD
3 pints (2L) milk (not skimmed)
fresh lemon juice
4 oz (120g) butter
1-2 Tbsps. rosewater
1½ beaten eggs
cinnamon, nutmeg

Heat the milk almost to boiling point, add lemon juice (½ to 1 lemon), and stir until it curdles. Allow to stand until cool and drain through a cheesecloth overnight. This should produce about 10oz (300g) of curd.

Beat the butter with the rosewater. Mix in the curds. Mix in beaten eggs, then grate in cinnamon to taste. Line an 8" (20cm) tin with pastry, fill with mx, sprinkle with nutmeg and bake at 190°C fir 25-30 min.

VICTORIA SPONGE
Guimaraens family recipe
Magdalena Gorrell Guimaraens

3 eggs
weight of eggs in butter, caster sugar and self-raising flour, each.
Jam
icing sugar

Cream the butter until it looks like whipped cream, add sugar and beat until white.

Add eggs, one at a time, followed by a good spoonful of flour, until all the flour is used. Beat thoroughly.

Turn into two 7" well-buttered and floured sandwich tins. Bake in a moderate oven 20-30 min. Turn out when cool, sandwich with jam and powder with icing sugar.

SAD CAKES

Sad Cake, widely known round Malton ad the Wolds, appears to be very similar to the Wensleydale Nodden cakes, only it is baked in one piece and then cut into sections, instead of being cut into shapes before baking. Sad Cake is a useful item to send out to the harvest field, ready buttered and cut into sections. For more formal occasions, the cake can be split and buttered and then sandwiched together with treacle. ***Susan Cook***

STAMFORD BRIDGE SPEAR OR PEAR PIES

September 1066, a great battle took place at Stamford Bridge. The English were endeavouring to cross the river at the old wooden bridge, but this was being held by one intrepid Norseman who stood in the centre of the bridge and defied all comers. At last one of the English hit upon a solution. He embarked in a small boat or coracle and drifted downstream till he was exactly under the bridge. He then thrust upwards through the holes in the bridge with his spear and swiftly dispatched the Norseman and so opened the bridge to his men. This feat was recalled for many years at the Stamford Bridge Feast which used to be held on the first Monday after September 19th. Spear or pear pies were made and sold. Apparently the pies were pastry boats filled with spiced hazel pears. Some say the stalk of the pear was left in place to represent the famous spear. Others say that an iron meat skewer was placed upright in the pastry boats. Yet another version was that the "pies" were more like flat cakes with the imprint of a skewer on the top. Although the original recipe is long lost, it seems most probable that the original pies were meat or savoury rather than sweet. Sugar was still unknown and honey was the only form of sweetening. ***Susan Cook***

NOTES

FISH DISHES

In Rotherham, South Yorkshire, a "fishcake" is a layer of fish between two slices of potato, battered and then deep fried. On the other hand, a fishcake 'down south' is mashed potato and fish, added spices and then fried. 'Up north', this is called a "rissole".

FISH CAKES or RISSOLES
Christina Flanigan, California

1 lb cooked fish
1 oz butter or margarine
8 oz mashed potatoes
2 eggs
salt and pepper
breadcrumbs

Remove skin and any bones and chop fish coarsely.

Melt the butter and add the fish, potatoes, yolk of 1 egg, salt and pepper to taste. Mix well to blend the fish and potatoes.

Shape into small flat cakes, brush with beaten egg, coat with the breadcrumbs and fry in hot fat.

ALTERNATIVE METHOD
The mixture may be shaped as one large cake and placed in a large greased tin. Brush with the beaten egg, sprinkle with breadcrumbs and bake for about 20 min in a 365°F oven.

FISH AND POTATO PUFF
Susan Cook, Westbank, B.C.

2 cups fish any kind
2 Tbsp finely chopped celery
2 cups mashed potato
2 Tbsp parsley
1 tsp salt
1 tsp minced onion
1 Tbsp lemon juice
2 Tbsp butter
3 eggs, separated

Grease bottom only of a medium-sized casserole dish.

Combine all together except eggs. Beat egg whites until they form stiff peaks. In a separate bowl, beat egg yolks until light. Add mixed ingredients then fold in beaten egg whites.

Pile carefully into casserole dish and bake at 350°F for 30-40 minutes.

Parsley sauce and niblet corn go nicely with this.

FRIED FISH IN BEER BATTER
Christina Flanigan, California

8 oz flour
salt to taste
2 eggs, separated
8 oz beer at room temperature
2 Tbsp oil (corn, peanut, vegetable)
2 lbs fish

BATTER
Place flour and salt in a mixing bowl and add the egg yolks. Start beating with a whisk. Stir in the beer and oil.

Cover and let stand until ready to use. When you are ready to use it, beat the egg whites until stiff and fold them into the batter.

Prepare the fish and pat as dry as possible. Use a deep fryer, start heating your favourite cooking oil or lard. Dip the fish in the batter and gently lower into the hot fat. Do not overcrowd the pan.

Allow to cook 2-3 min, turning them over until golden brown. Repeat until all the fish is cooked.

HOMEMADE FISH PASTE
Ann Newman, Somerset

½ lb cooked fish
1 tsp vinegar
1 oz flour
cayenne pepper
2-3 oz melted butter
1 tsp anchovy essence
pinch of ground mace

Free the fish from skin and bone, then put in a strong basin with most of the butter and the seasonings. Pound the mixture well until it is smooth, then rub it through a sieve. Pack it into small jars and run the remainder of the melted butter over the top to seal. Keep cool and use within 2-3 days.

GOOD FRIDAY FISH PIE
Susan Cook, Westbank, B.C.

Boil or steam some woof or ling and remove the flesh from the bones and skin. Cut some lean ham into neat pieces (uncooked). Slice some hard boiled eggs.

Put into a greased pie dish, alternate layers, together with a little of the liquid from the fish.

When the dish is full, cover it with an ordinary short crust pastry and put in a hot oven till the pastry is done.

MRS. CHEADLES' SALMON PASTE
Martyn Gleaden, Wath-Upon-Dearne
From a 1900 notebook by Mary Duckett, with kind permission from the Duckett family in Sykehouse.

1 large tin of salmon
1 oz breadcrumbs
1 oz butter
3 Tbsp vinegar
½ tsp mustard
salt and pepper, mixed

To be well pounded into a paste.

SALMON LOAF
Susan Cook, Westbank, B.C.

1 can salmon (7 ½ oz)
1 tsp parsley
1 cup bread crumbs
½ minced onion
1 egg
½ tsp each salt and pepper
½ cup milk

Mix all together and put in loaf pan. Bake at 375°F for 45 minutes.

STUFFED PLAICE
Susan Cook, Westbank, B.C.

1½ lb plaice fillets
1½ Tbsp butter or margarine
3 oz breadcrumbs
1 Tbsp chopped parsley
salt and pepper
few drops lemon juice
1 egg

FOR SHRIMP SAUCE
¾ oz margarine
1 oz flour
½ pint milk
seasoning to taste
½ picked shrimp

Chop butter into breadcrumbs, add parsley and seasoning and mix with the egg. Wrap a piece of this stuffing into each fillet and place them in a greased pie dish. Cover with greased paper and cook in a moderate oven for 20 min.

For the sauce, melt the fat and stir in the flour. Gradually add the milk and stir till the sauce thickens.

Add seasoning to taste and the shrimp. Pour the sauce over the fillets before serving and garnish with slices of lemon and chopped parsley.

YORKSHIRE HERRING PIE
Kathleen Allott Guimaraens
ex-Rotherham, now Northern Portugal

4 fresh herrings
1 shallot
4 potatoes, blanched, whole
salt and pepper
2 sour apples
1 gill (½ cup)water

Wash and bone herrings, cut into fillets and soak for a little while in salted water. Slice the potatoes thinly. Butter a pie dish generously and line round with potato.

Chop the shallot and the apples very fine and mix together. Place a layer of herring, season and cover with a layer of apple mix. Repeat until the dish is full. Finish with a layer of potato slices. Add liquid, cover and cook in a moderate oven (350°F) for 45min-1 hour.

WHITEBAIT
Traditional recipe

1 pint whitebait
seasoned flour
oil or far for deep frying

Pick over whitebait but do not wash fish. Roll lightly in seasoned flour, a little at a time.

Dip in handfuls into hot fat and fry for 2-3 minutes in a basket and drain on paper towel.

When all the fish have been fried, put them altogether in the basket and fry another 1-2 min until crisp.

NOTES

MEAT DISHES

FAGGOTS or SAVOURY DUCKS

Someone asked about Faggots, also known as Savoury Ducks. This recipe, enjoyed all over Yorkshire, is yet another example of how ingenious women, forced by chronic poverty to buy the cheapest of foods, were able to create tasty and nourishing dishes to sustain our ancestors, without whom we would not be here to argue about things today. You will notice this recipe calls for a pig's caul. Don't ask. Make the faggots without it.

1 lb pound pig's liver
a pig's caul (optional)
2 medium onions
1 egg
salt and pepper
4 oz fat pork
pinch of basil
pinch grated nutmeg
pinch of thyme
½ heaping tsp powdered sage
Breadcrumbs

Slice the liver, onions and pork thinly. Put in a saucepan with the thyme, sage, basil, salt, pepper and nutmeg and barely cover with water. Simmer for ½ hour, then strain off the liquid and save for the gravy.

Mince the contents of the stewpan finely. Add the beaten egg and sufficient breadcrumbs to make into a fairly firm mixture and mix thoroughly.

Form into balls and enclosed each one in a piece of caul. Place in baking tin and add a little gravy. Bake at 400°F until nicely browned.

Serve with a good thickened gravy. If preferred, the mixture can be pressed into a well-greased baking tin and marked into squares. Cover with caul and cut into squares after cooking. 6 servings.

BRADFORD HASH
Ann Newman, Somerset

"My mom used to make this but she always added uncooked potatoes on to the top and cooked it until the potatoes were tender and browned."

1 lb cooked beef or mutton, sliced thinly
1 small carrot
½ small turnip
1 scant Tbsp flour
½ cup Yorkshire relish or similar sauce
1 small onion
½ teacup mushroom ketchup or puréed mushrooms
seasoning
1 bunch mixed herbs, parsley, thyme and bay Leaf

Using a pint of water, make a stock (with either bones or stock cubes) add vegetables and herbs and cook until tender.

Melt some oil or fat. Peel and chop onion and fry until brown. Stir in flour gradually. Keep stirring and add the mushroom ketchup, sauce and seasoning.

Add the strained stock a little at a time and stirring well. Put in meat slices and heat thoroughly.

BOILED SALTED BEEF AND DUMPLINGS.
Magdalena Gorrell Guimaraens

"This recipe, a classical way of preparing beef, was given me by my father-in-law's cousin, Patrick Guimaraens. It was handed down to him by his mother, a Lethbridge, whose ancestors were Thorntons, although I am not sure whether they connect with the Yorkshire Thorntons or not."

BRINE FOR SALTING THE MEAT
1 gallon water
1 oz saltpetre
2½ lbs coarse salt
1 lb brown sugar
Boil for 15 minutes, skim and cool.

THE MEAT
2-4 lbs silverside or topside of beef

Rub the piece of meat to be pickled with salt and leave for 24 hours. Dry and pack closely in a jar or vat. Pour the brine over the meat, putting a weight on top to hold the meat down under the liquid. Keep for at least 3 days.

DUMPLINGS
(See recipe for Suet Dumplings, under Savouries).

1 medium onion into which a clove has been stuck
5 medium whole onions
1 bay leaf
5 medium carrots, quartered
small bunch of parsley
2 turnips, quartered
sprig of thyme
½ dozen peppercorns

Put the salted beef into a large pan and cover with unsalted water. Bring slowly to the boil, skimming often. Add herbs, peppercorns and cloved onion.

Half cover the pan with a lid and simmer for 1½ hours. Remove herbs and add vegetables. Cook slowly 40-50 min until the vegetables are just tender. Add dumplings, cover the pan and cook a further 15-20 min.

Serve with horseradish sauce.

CHRISTMAS PIE
A Victorian recipe
Tana Willis Johnson, Gloucestershire

One turkey, one goose, one fowl, one pigeon, a little sausage meat, some forcemeat, six or eight hardboiled eggs, half an ounce of pepper, half an ounce of salt and some savoury jelly or gravy, enough raised pie crust.

Bone a turkey, a goose, a fowl and a pigeon and season the insides of each with pepper and salt mixed together.

Put the goose inside the turkey, the fowl inside the goose, the pigeon inside that, filling the interstices with a little forcemeat, sausage meat and six or eight hardboiled eggs cut into three.

Sew up the turkey to give the appearance of a whole bird and lay it in a thick crust. Cut or mark out a lid at the top, brush it over with the beaten yolk of eggs and ornament the top and sides.

(Roast in a medium oven until done, approximately 3-4 hours.)

It will keep a long time as the crust is not to be eaten but merely forms a case for the poultry.

HOW TO JUG A HARE
Susan Cook, Westbank, B.C.

1 hare
1 large onion stuck with 4 cloves
1 tsp mixed herbs
2 oz butter
2 oz flour
thin strip of lemon rind
seasoning
enough stock or water to cover

Skin, clean and wipe hare very thoroughly., joint neatly, dip joints into seasoned flour and fry till well browned.

Place hare, onion, herbs and lemon rind in a large casserole or pan. Cover well with stock or water and fit lid tightly.

Cook gently in a moderate over for 3 hours.

An hour before dishing up, add forcemeat balls and a couple of glasses of Port Wine if desired.

MEAT AND FISH PASTE

Meat and fish when pounded and mixed with other ingredients and flavourings, give a smooth paste which is good for sandwich fillings, canapé spreads, etc.

Many commercially made brands ae sod so these may be stored unopened for some time as they contain preservatives.

Delicious fish and meat pastes may also be made at home, but these should be prepared as required and used up within a day or two.

See recipes for fish paste under Fish Dished.

LIVER PASTE or PATÉ
Ann Newman, Somerset

"This makes an excellent hors d'oeuvre and is very good as a sandwich spread, combined with watercress or sliced cucumber."

¾ lb veal liver
½ pint of stock or water
1 oz plain flour
salt and pepper
1 oz dripping
a bouquet garni
1 sliced onion
a little melted butter

Cut the liver into slices, removing the pipes and coat with flour.

Melt the dripping in a saucepan or casserole and fry the liver lightly. Add the onion, sauté for a few minutes, then stir in the remaining flour.

Add the stock and seasonings and bring to boil, add bouquet garni tied in muslin, cover and simmer gently until very tender (3/4 to 1 hour).

Remove the bag of herbs, lift the liver from the sauce and pass it through a fine mincer then sieve. Add more seasonings if necessary, with enough gravy to make a soft paste.

Pack into small pots, cover at once with a little melted butter and leave to cool. Keep in a cold place and use within 2-3 days.

Serve with freshly made toast and fresh butter.

PORK PIE (1)
Martyn Gleaden, Wath-Upon-Dearne
From a 1900 notebook by Mary Duckett, with kind permission from the Duckett family in Sykehouse.

PASTE
7 lbs flour
3 lbs lard
2 oz baking powder
1 handful salt
1 quart boiling water

Rub half the lard in the flour and boil the remainder with the water. Make a hole in the flour, pour all the water and lard in and mix up at once.

MEAT SEASONING
4 oz salt
2 oz pepper
To every 12 lbs meat

PORK PIE (2)
Ann Newman, Somerset

"This recipe for pork pie came from my Great-Aunt Mary's collection and was taken from a booklet of Yorkshire recipes published in the 1920s (guessing from the adverts)."

PASTRY
¾ lb/3 USA cups flour
5 oz/1¼ USA cups lard
¾ tsp salt
About ¼ pints/5 fluid oz water or
    milk and water mixed.

Boil lard with water then stir into flour gradually and knead to a smooth light paste, cut off about ¼ of it and set to keep warm.

Make the remainder into a ball, then gradually work out the centre, getting the sides as high as possible up the sides of a tin with a loose bottom, then fill with pie meat and wet the inside of the upper edge of the case.

Roll out the remainder (make a hole in the middle) and cover pie, press edges together and pinch them all round.

Decorate the top with shapes of pastry. Brush over with beaten egg and bake 1½ hours. Before quite cold, fill up with seasoned gravy.

FILLING
1½ lb pork
1 Tbsp water
½ oz salt
¼ oz pepper

Cut the meat up finely and mix well with seasoning and water. Half a teaspoonful sage may be added if liked.

REGARDING BUTCHERS
Denise Oyston, Huddersfield

"There used to be a butcher's in Barnsley who made award-winning pork pies and black puddings. We used to buy pies on a Saturday when doing our shopping. Sometimes they were still warm and you had to be careful carrying them, otherwise the jelly ran out.

I can still remember the taste of those pies. I was a great tragedy when his shops closed down.

There was a good pie shop on Rvegate in Bradford. The queues at Christmas went on forever and they did a good brawn."

POTTED MEAT
(An old Christmas recipe)
Susan Cook, Westbank, B.C.

3 pork hocks
2 lbs stewing beef (off the shank)
salt and pepper
2 tsp whole mixed pickling spices

Wash meats quickly. Put into soup kettle, cover with cold water, bring to a boil and simmer gently for 3 hours.

Remove and drain meat then put through meat chopper. Set aside.

Boil bones as long as necessary to extract gelatine. Strain.

Add spices tied in a cheesecloth bag and continue cooking until liquid is reduced to half the original amount.

Lift out spices return meat to kettle, add salt and pepper to taste. Mix thoroughly. Turn mixture into bowls which have been wet with cold water. Chill until firm.

Serve alone or with sliced turkey.

SMALL RAISED YORKSHIRE PORK PIES
(A Victorian recipe)
Tana Willis Johnson, Gloucestershire

2 lbs neck of pork
¼ lb butter
¼ lb suet
1 lb flour
1 tsp sugar
pepper and salt.

Chop a quarter of a pound of suet very fine, mix it with a quarter of a pound of butter and a pound of fine dry flour.

Put it in a stewpan over a slow fire to become hot and the suet and the butter are melted.

Knead it into a very stiff paste and set it before the fire covered over with a cloth until required.

Cut the pork into the smallest pieces and season them highly with pepper, salt and a tsp of powdered sage.

Divide the paste into as many pieces as you think fit, reserving some for the tops. Raise them into round forms, fill them with the small pieces of seasoned pork, cover the tops, pinch them round with your thumb and finger and bake them in a very hot brick oven.

TOAD IN THE HOLE

"Eileen was asking about toad in the hole, Indeed, that is what you call piggies in a blanket, Eileen (in the US pigs in blankets means hot dogs wrapped in pastry). For this you'll need traditional British style 'bangers' available at British specialty stores – or use some good sage-flavoured sausage, if possible. Our working-class sausages are called 'bangers' because they often explode nicely when well cooked. (You can defuse bangers by pricking them with a fork.)"

1 lb bangers or similar sausages
Yorkshire pudding batter
1 oz/2 Tbsp dripping or lard
good gravy

Make batter, let stand for 1 hour.

Heat oven to 425°F. Heat dripping or lard in a Yorkshire pudding (lasagne) tin until just smoking.

Put the sausages in the tin, bake about 5 minutes. Pour in all the batter and cook for another 30 min.

TRICIA'S VERY OWN STEAK AND KIDNEY PUDDING
Tricia Backhouse, Huntsville, Ontario

SUET PASTRY
Make suet pastry using self-raising flour suet and water. Use half the amount of suet to flour, e.g., 6 oz flour, 3 oz suet, salt and pepper. Mix together an use cold water enough to make an elastic dough. Rest about 20 min while you prepare the filling.

FILLING

Chop up 1 lb of stewing beef and 1 beef kidney. Remove the white muscle from the kidney. Soak the kidney in salt water for 10 min.

Take ¼ cup seasoned flour, put into a plastic bag and shake eat and kidney in the flour.

Prepare a 2 pint pudding basin by buttering it well. Take ¾ of pastry roll out and line basin. Put in meat mixture with a little chopped onion. Add enough cold water to reach almost to the top of the meat.

Roll out pastry lid and put on top. Cover with buttered grease-proof paper; tie down around the rim and then cover with aluminium foil.

Steam over boiling water for approximately 4½ hours, topping up boiling water as necessary,

VARIATION

"I sometimes put in some mushrooms and sprinkle in some herbs. May also be flavoured with Worcestershire Sauce,"

TRIPE
Marge Cambridge

"In some parts of the country only undressed tripe is sold by the butchers. Where this is the case, the tripe should be washed and scraped in several waters, and all far and discoloured parts removed. Put it then in a deep pan, cover with cold water, bring to the boil and throw this water away. Repeat 2 or 3 times until the tripe smells quite sweet. Cover with water and simmer from 8 to 10 hours until it is tender. After that it can be used in any number of ways."

BRAISED TRIPE
Marge Cambridge, Mission, B.C.

Prepare tripe as before. Cut into slices and on each put some forcemeat and a slice of thin bacon. Tie with string. Braise these on a bed of vegetables for 2½ to 3 hours or even more. Serve dished on a border of mashed potato, with brown gravy poured round and garnished with some of the braised vegetables.

TRIPE PIE
Mal Walker's Yorkshire
Dad's Own Recipe.

Stew tripe until tender then leave to jelly in the liquor.

Line a pie dish with pastry, put 2 or 3 rashers of bacon on the bottom, then put in the tripe. Add jelly gravy, 2 or 3 pieces of butter and season with salt and pepper.

Pour in half a cupful of brown gravy and cover with pastry.

Bake until brown.

TRIPE - RAW
Christine Harris, Auckland,
New Zealand

"Yorkshiremen traditionally eat tripe raw, but soaked in vinegar.!"

Pat Fisher, Auckland, New Zealand

"My grandmother used to cook it in milk with a good lashing of onions, however I picked up my taste for tripe from my grandfather – just soak it in malt vinegar and go for it."

Martyn Gleaden, Wath-upon-Dearne

"A traditional way to eat tripe in Barnsley/Wombell/Darfield was to eat it simply with sale, vinegar and pepper. I had to eat this slimy, revolting mess as a child – I still shudder when I think about it!"

TRIPE - STUFFED
Susan Cook, Westbank, B.C.

A piece of tripe large enough to fold
breadcrumbs
sliced bacon
boiled onions
mixed herbs (sage, thyme bay leaf)
salt and pepper

Make a stuffing of breadcrumbs and boiled onions. Season with herbs, salt and pepper, to taste. Spread a thick layer of this over half of the tripe. Fold over the other half and sew the edges.

Place in a greased tin with a few slices of bacon on top and bake at 350°F for about 1 hour.

Serve with brown gravy.

TRIPE WITH MILK AND ONIONS
Pam Smith, Brisbane, Australia

"When I was a child in the WRY, we used to buy tripe that was ready to eat, from the Tripe dresser's shop. My Dad used to buy it for his supper; just add pepper and salt and vinegar and eat it with bread and butter.

When we had tripe and onions, my Mum bought the tripe (plain honeycomb or thick seam, which I think was pig tripe and was grey and folded from a thick ridge) from the tripe shop, cut it into bite-sized pieces and finely sliced an onion with it, cooked it gently for about 20 min in milk, which she thickened with cornflour. We ate it with bread and butter and seasoning to taste.

Here in Australia I've been unable to buy thick seam, have to search for honeycomb tripe, but plain tripe is common at any butcher's.

It has to be boiled in salted water for at least 2 hours until tender, then cut up with onions and stewed in milk and thickened – and it still doesn't taste as good as it did in Yorkshire!"

VEAL "BIRDS"
with Raisin Stuffing
Ann Scott, Bangley, West Yorkshire

"From my Granma's recipe book (ca. 1900)." Sent in by Mrs. Lilley, Castleford.

1 lb veal
3 oz raisins
yolk of one egg
8 oz stale breadcrumbs
2 oz butter
a little suet
hot water
pepper and salt

Mix well together breadcrumbs, raisins, pepper and salt and beaten yolk of egg. Pour over butter previously melted in a cupful of hot water.

Cut veal into 6 square pieces, put a spoonful of stuffing in the centre of each, roll up and tie.

Season with salt and pepper and place in a roasting tin with a piece of suet on each "bird", add hot water to cover the bottom of the dish. Roast until tender.

YORKSHIRE PIE
A Victorian Recipe
Tana Willis Johnson, Gloucestershire

"Bone a goose and a large fowl. Fill the latter with a stuffing made of minced ham or tongue, veal, suet, parsley, pepper, salt and two eggs; or for a more highly seasoned stuffing, minced ham, veal, suet, onion, sweet herbs, lemon peel, mixed spices, cayenne, salt – worked into a paste with a couple of eggs.

Sew up the fowl, truss it and stew it for twenty minutes along with the goose in some good stock and close stewpan.

Put the fowl with the goose and place the goose in a pie mould which has been lined with good hot water paste. Let the goose repose on a cushion of stuffing in the midst of the liquor in which he has bee stewed.

Surround him in the pie with slices of parboiled tongue and pieces of pigeon, partridge or hare. Fill the vacancies with more stuffing, put on a good layer of butter, roof it with paste.

Bake it for three hours and consume it either hot or cold. These pies are sometimes made of enormous size, containing every variety of poultry or game, one within another and side by side.

MORE REMARKS ON PORK PIES

"I am sorry if, to some people, the subject of warm pork pies ranks alongside 'squirrels' as a subject that should not be discussed on the [*sic.* genealogy] list, but to me warm pork pies and Yorkshire Genealogy are facets of the same diamond, they should be considered as the number one life reviving item after those cold wet stomps around graveyards looking for ancestors."

Colin Pikles, Maidstone, Kent

"I spent two summer holidays in the mid fifties, in my mid teens, working in the pie manufacturing room of Wright's Pork Butchers in Goodramgate, York. Started at 5:30 am except for the Ebor Cup meeting. On Ebor Day itself we started at 2 am and by 9 am had produced 125,000 individual pork pies and over 10,000 larger ones known as stand pies. We produced another 125,000 small pies before knocking off early at 2 pm.

They made a few other things in the same room. Probably would not be tolerated under present-day hygiene conditions. They also butchered their pigs "out 't back". Stun them, haul them up by the hind legs and cut their throats so they would bleed properly. Catch it of course, for black pudding.

I didn't want to advertise recent outlets generally, but there are a couple of places in Adelaide you can get a passable pork pie (and one for black pudding, white pudding, haslet and faggots)."

Rowland Bruce, Adelaide, S. Australia

"Pork pies were readily on sale in Huddersfield and when my parents had a fish and chip shop in Linthwaite in the late 40's, mum used to boil up those mushy peas and sell pies and peas.

We also bought a variety of these pies for special occasions – large ones which could be cut in pieces and served with salad. You could eat them hot or cold with HP Sauce. They went well sandwiches too.

I certainly miss them. In Adelaide you can buy them (nothing like as good of course) and they don't refer to them as 'Pork Pies' but 'English Pies'. Australian meat pies are totally different."

Jean Spence, Adelaide, S. Australia

BAG, COW HEEL AND OTHER QUAINT FARE

Norman Backhouse **illuminates us:**

"Some of us, further removed from our Yorkshire roots, did not realise that Yorkies ate quite so much tripe and in so may different ways. Whereas we knew of some people's predilection for liver, heart, sweetbreads and the ilk, and although Magdalena frequently cooks calf's foot and pig's trotters back home, we never in our wildest imagination eve consider 'bag'.

Cow Heel is literally that. The heel part of a cow's hoof, but I'm not sure whether bull heel is also valid. I never saw it mentioned at the local tripe shop on Spital Hill Sheffield from say 1942 until maybe late 1950s. It's ugly looking, messy looking, stuff but if stewed with suitable seasonings, it makes an excellent nourishing meal.

Bag is cow udder and this certainly does not have an equivalent on bulls. I recall that this would be eaten uncooked with lots of salt, pepper and genuine brown vinegar (not the brewed condiment variety) Another excellent meal.

These meals came into their glory during the war when there was sometimes ten pence (not 10p but 10d) of meat per person per week and tripe ad the like were not rationed.

That reminds me that you probably do not know of bag balm. This is an ointment which dairy farmers would apply to the udders of their cows to deal with inflamed conditions. It was a fairly local reedy typically concocted by farmers who found James Herriott just a little pricey. Surprisingly enough, a well known recording female artist uses this as some kind of complexion softening cosmetic. It seems so successful that there are occasionally shortages of this balm for its intended purpose.

Mrs. Beeton tells us that 'Ox-feet [*sic.* cow heel] may be dressed in various ways, stewed in gravy or plainly boiled and served with melted butter. When plainly boiled, the liquor will answer for making sweet or relishing jellies and also to give richness to soups or gravies'."

BAG
Susan Buffrey, Ipswich, Suffolk

"Cow heel, I believe, is still very much a Londoner's delicacy. Bag, however, is definitely a Yorkshireman's delight. It is bought cooked and then served freshly washed with salt and vinegar. My husband Martin, always buys some when we are both 'back home' in Yorkshire. His eyes light up when he goes to a market in Sheffield and can buy bag.

BACON AND COW HEEL PUDDING
Ann Garrison, ex-Harrogate, now Reading, Berkshire

"This is a true savoury pie, possibly developed from the earlier Medley Pie which as the name implies, was a combination of ingredients. The Derbyshire Medley Pie also included onions and sage ad was served with a jog of hot vinegar."

¾ lb lean bacon rashers
1 cow heel, dressed
1 onion studded with cloves
1 pint meat stock, preferably beef
salt and pepper
½ lb savoury shortcrust pastry
1 egg
Oven 350°F, Gas Mark 4; 1 hour

Put the cow heel in a large pan, add the onion and cover with stock; season with salt and pepper.

Bring to the boil, cover and simmer for about 3 hours or until tender.

Remove the cow heel, strip off the meat and cut into cubes. Wrap the meat in the bacon rashers.

Place in a 2 pint pie dish and cover with pastry. Brush with beaten egg and bake for 1 hour.

Serves 6-8 portions.

BEEF AND COW HEEL MOLD
Susan Cook, Westbank, B.C.

1 lb lean stewing meat
½ a cow heel
salt and pepper to taste
1 pint cold water

Put the beef and the cow heel into a pan, add salt and pepper. Pour over the cold water. Put on the lid and simmer for 3 hours, adding more water if needed but keeping the liquid to one pint in the pan.

When cooked, remove the bones and put the beef and cow heel into a large dish. Chop into shreds with a sharp knife.

Pour the hot stock over all the mix well. Place into small basins, previously rinsed in cold water.

Leave to set in a cool place.

BOILED COW HEEL
Joy Ellis, ex-Leeds, now Somerset

2 cow heels
water or stock to cover
fat for greasing
25 g butter or dripping
25 g flour
1 Tbsp chopped parsley
salt and pepper to taste

Wash the cow heels and blanch for 6-8 min in boiling water. Drain and place in saucepan with water or stock to cover. Bring to a boil, reduce heat, cover and simmer for 3 hours.

Just before the end of cooking, melt butter or dripping in a saucepan, add flour, stirring constantly.

Pour off 500 ml of the liquid the cow heels cooked in and gradually stir into the roux. Add parsley.

Drain heels and remove bones. Arrange pieces on a serving dish, cover with hot sauce and serve.

"When I lived in Scarborough there used to be a tripe shop in the market square, where they sold cow heels, tripe udder, pig's trotters, chitterlings and sweet-breads."

COW HEEL PASTY
Ann Garrison, ex-Harrogate, now Reading, Berkshire

3 cow heels, dressed
¾ lb shin of beef
1 pint brown meat stock, preferably beef
salt and pepper
¾ lb savoury shortcrust pastry
1 egg
Oven 400°C, Gas Mark 6; 45 min

Have the cow heel split by the butcher. Put the heels and the shin of beef in a pan, cover with stock, add salt and pepper and simmer for about 3 hours.

Strip the meat from the heels and cut it and the beef into 1 in cubes.

Line an 8" pie plate with half the pastry. Spoon over the meat filling and cover the remaining. Brush with beaten egg ad bake 45 min.

(The Bacon and Cow Heel Pudding recipe and the above recipe for Cow Heel Pasty are from a book edited by Lizzie Boyd in 1976, the product of a research program at Strathclyde University, with recipes from all over the country. The authors of the recipes are not credited.)

MRS. BEATON'S FRIED OX-FEET or COW HEEL
Alan Longbottom, Pudsey

"Originally published as number 639 in 1859-61, in monthly supplements. First published as one volume in 1861 entitled "The Book of Household Management." This recipe is from the Enlarged First Edition published in UK in 1982 by Chancellor Press, p. 297."

ox-feet
the yolk of 1 egg
breadcrumbs, parsley, boiling butter
salt and cayenne pepper to taste

Wash, scald and thoroughly clean the feet, and cut them into pieces about 2in long; have ready some fine bread crumbs mixed with a little minced parsley, cayenne and salt; dip the pieces of heel into the yolk of egg, sprinkle them with the bread crumbs, and fry them until of a nice brown in boiling butter. Time 15 min.

STEWED OX CHEEK
Joy Ellis, ex-Leeds, now Somerset

A boned ox cheek, soaked in salted cold water for at least 12 hrs, wash in warm water. Cur into pieces, put in pan, cover with cold water, baring to the boil, and skim.

Add 2 chopped onions, 2 diced carrots, 1 turnip, 12 peppercorns, bouquet garni and salt. Simmer, covered, for 2 hours or until tender. Strain, keeping liquor.

Melt 1 oz butter, add 2 oz flour, in a pan and cook over gentle heat until lightly browned. Gradually add liquor, stirring constantly, until you have a medium-thick sauce. Lower heat and simmer 10 min.

Add some sherry to taste, then some lemon juice and season to taste. Add the meat pieces and reheat briefly. Garnish with strips of carrot and turnip. Use remaining liquor to make a soup.

TIPS FOR ROASTING A STANDING BEEF RIB
David Hinde, Roscoe, Illinois
"Some of this is from my Sheffield-born Granny, Maud Machin Hinde."

For roasting a standing rib, a leg o' lamb, or a pork loin, I rub the fat side of the roast with freshly ground black pepper for all three. For lamb (and sometimes a beef roast), I cut incisions through the fat side and insert slivers of fresh peeled garlic cloves; and for both lamb and pork I also rub the fat side with some dried sage and thyme. Fresh rosemary is also quite nice, I think. Put the roast on a rack in a roasting pan.

Preheat the oven to 425°F (220°C) and when it's ready, put the roasting pan in the oven for 20 minutes Turn the heat down to 350-375°F (180-190°C) and roast to the desired level of doneness – I always use an internal meat thermometer inserted so that it does not come in contact with any bone, which would throw the reading off.

A nice variation if you happen to have two boneless pork loins, is to layer some dried apricot halves along the fatless side of one of them, match up the fatless side of the other on top, then tie the two loins together in 3 or 4 places, and proceed with normal roasting.

Parboiled peeled potato quarters can be roasted alongside the meat if you wish, for any roast. In that case, omit the roasting rack and just place the meat and potatoes right in the pan.

With the old-fashioned way, aside from the humongous cuts of meat that were sometimes cooked in very wealthy homes, the roast was first seared in a pan on top of the stove until light brown on all sides before putting it on a rack in a moderate oven, usually part of a wood-burning stove. The cook would pour a cup of boiling stock over the meat and cover it until done, basting it from time to time. The fat on the meat was rarely trimmed before and this, together with the stock, would make the most wonderful dripping ad gravy.

An avowed carnivore myself, I like my meat 'on the leash' so-to-speak. I find that first braising the meat quickly in a heavy pan and then baking it 10 mn per pound makes the perfect roast. For guests who prefer their meat more well done, a minute or two's microwaving of the sliced meat works beautifully."

TIMETABLE FOR ROASTING FRESH MEAT

	Weight (lbs)	Oven Temperature	Approx. Min per lb.
BEEF			
Standing Ribs	6-8	300°F	
Rare			18-20
Medium			22-25
Well done			27-30
PORK			
Loin – centre	3-4	350°F	35-40
Shoulder, whole	12-14		30-35
LAMB			
Leg	6½ - 7½ ~	300°F	30-35
Shoulder	3-4		40-45

PICKLES AND SAUCES
PICKLES

PICCALILLI
Traditional Recipe

1 heaping Tbsp flour
3 gills vinegar
1 level Tbsp sugar
1 cup pickling spice
small tin of mustard
¼ tsp powdered turmeric
1 lb onions
1 lb cauliflower
½ cucumber

Mix flour, sugar, mustard and powdered turmeric with a little vinegar. Tie pickling spice in a cheesecloth bag and boil with rest of vinegar for 5 min. Pour in paste and simmer for 5 min.. Remove bag. Add chopped cauliflower, onion and cucumber to the liquid. Stir for another 5 min. Cool and bottle.

GREEN APPLE CHUTNEY
Magdalena Gorrell Guimaraens, Northern Portugal

2 lbs green apples
1 lb onions
½ lb seedless raisins
2 lbs brown sugar
1 cup Worcestershire sauce

Chop apples and onions into small pieces. Put into a heavy pan and add all the other ingredients. Simmer over a slow heat until soft, stirring often, about 30 minutes or until dark brown. Put into jars and seal.

YORKHIRE RELISH
Jude Kettlewell, born Ilkley, now in Northumberland

"Extracted from my Great-Grandmother's handwritten recipe book from about 1880."

½ oz cloves
½ oz cayenne pods
1 oz peppercorns

Put into a pa with ½ pint of water, boil for 20 min then add ¼ pint vinegar, 3 oz salt, 8 oz moist sugar and 1 penn'orth of burnt sugar. Let all boil together for 2-3 min, strain and it is already for use.

SAUCES

BROWN GRAVY
David Hinde, Roscoe, Illinois

"For a standard brown gravy, I just use some of the roast's drippings (skimmed of the fat, which is saved for Yorkshire puddings). When the roast is done, remove and cover it with a piece of aluminium foil – then pour a cup or more of boiling water into the roasting pan, crape all the yummy bits loose and pour into a fat separator. This liquid is then used along with the water used in cooking the potatoes and vegetables, in the standard Bisto recipe.

If the roast you are doing doesn't produce much in the way of drippings, then supplement what you have with butter or lard (NOT margarine).

We have to do that when we prepare a second pudding for the leftover roast anyway. You have to watch the melting process of the butter a bit more carefully, however, as you don't want it to blacken before pouring the batter in.

HORSERADISH SAUCE
Handed down by Patrick Guimaraens

1-2 heaping Tbsp freshly grated
　　horseradish, more for hotter sauce
1 tsp vinegar
1 tsp lemon juice
½ tsp mustard
½ cup thick cream
sugar, salt and pepper to taste

Mix all the ingredients together, except the cream. Whip the cream until stiff and add the mixed ingredients. Adjust the seasonings.

MINT AND CUCUMBER SAUCE FOR LAMB
Anthony Taylor-Dawes, Northern Spain

large handful fresh mint leaves
2 Tbsp sugar
½ cup finely chopped cucumber
1 cup vinegar
1 cup boiling water

Chop the mint leaves finely and pound in a mortar with 1 Tbsp sugar. Add the rest of the sugar and the boiling water to dissolve.

Add vinegar and chopped cucumber. Leave to rest 1-2 hours before serving.

ONION GRAVY
David Hinde, Roscoe, Illinois

"For an onion gravy, I sauté one chopped medium onion in 4 Tbsp (60g) butter in a medium-sized sauce pan.

Then make a medium white sauce by adding 4 Tbsp flour stirred in until slightly browned (over medium-low heat) then add 2 cups milk.

Stir until thickened. I generally add a teaspoon or so of dry mustard, just after adding the milk to the pan.

PRESERVES AND JAMS

A WORD OF CAUTION

Many people will probably try out these jams who have never done any canning before and may figure it's alright to just pour them into any clean, empty jar that they have around. These jars should be sterilized and made of glass. It is also preferable to use the proper canning jars (Mason jars) with two-piece lids that will provide a proper seal. These should also be thoroughly washed in hot soapy water and then sterilized, ***Aileen Power, Ontario***

TIPS

Since some fruits are just more naturally sweet than others, equal sugar may be too sweet for some tastes. Perhaps a small amount of lemon could be added to reduce that flavour. In today's cooking, many use a product such as Certo to thicken/jell the fruit, but then it may not be the way you remember your grandma making her jams Although perhaps healthier if not all sugar! If you are new to jam making and use the Certo method, you will find much less boiling time is required and you will have more jam from each batch. This is a Canadian tip and not a genuine Yorkie one! ***June Ridsdale, Vancouver***

APPLE, PLUM or GREENGAGE JAM
Judith Lyon, Cronulla, NSW Australia

After taking away the stones from the fruit and cutting out any blemishes, cook over a slow fire in a clean stewpan with half a pint of water, When scalded, rub the fruit through a hair sieve.

To every pound of pulp, measure 1 lb of sifted loaf sugar. Cook in a preserving pan over a brisk fire and when it boils, skim well and add the kernels of the apricots and ½ oz of bitter almonds, blanched. Boil for an additional 15 min, stirring constantly. Store away in pots in the usual manner.

BLANKET JAM
An 1820s recipe
Sylvia Blenkin

Called 'Blanket' jam because it covers the method for making jam with every fruit.

Boil the berries with a tiny amount of water, until all the juice has come out of them. Put them through a sieve and add an equal amount of sugar to the juice. Boil until it begins to set and jar it.

BRUCE'S JAM MAKING MADE EASY
Magdalena Gorrell Guimaraens, Northern Portugal

"Being of good Yorkshire stock, my husband hated seeing anything going to waste, let alone the surplus apples and oranges from the trees in his orchard and tomatoes from the vegetable patch. He even sometimes got carried away when he went to the market, bringing back kilos of other fruit that struck his fancy!

Given the chance, he would invade my kitchen and make jams and marmalades of all sorts. Over the years, he developed (with a little help from me) the easiest possible method of making them into jam. Needless to say, these were the days when I took the day off and left the kitchen – and the cleaning up – to him!"

Measure equal weights of fruit and granulated sugar. Wash the fruit well, cut out any worms or other bugs and cut into small pieces.

Put the lot into a heavy aluminium pot and boil until the juice begins to set. Some fruit, such as pears and tomatoes, will need a little pectin to help them set. You can vary the taste by adding ground cinnamon, cloves, ginger or allspice.

Pour into sterilised hot jars and seal.

GOOSEBERRY JAM
Pauline Lane, Huddersfield
In an old, old cookbook belonging to the White Horse Inn, Fishergate, Doncaster.

Take your gooseberries when they are at their biggest and pilk them and putt them in a stoup and sett them among boyling water till they be tender then putt them throu a fine search and putt and equall wrought of suggar and boyle it to the consistence of a marmalet and box it up.

LEMON CURD (1)
Mrs. J. Smith, Halifax

250 g caster sugar
rind of 3 lemons
2 eggs
juice of 2 large lemons
100 g butter or margarine

Grate rind carefully, removing just the yellow zest but none of the white pith. If using loaf sugar, rub this over the lemons until all the yellow as been removed. Squeeze the juice from the fruit. Put all the ingredients – except eggs – into a double saucepan or basin and cook, over hot water, stirring from time to time until the margarine and sugar have melted.

Add the well-beaten eggs and continue cooking until the mixture coats the back of a wooden spoon. Pour into jars and seal tightly.

LEMON CURD (2)
Anne Garrison, ex-Halifax, now Reading, Berkshire

The microwave is ideal for lemon curd, saving time dramatically compared with the conventional method. The flavour is good, but the texture is perhaps a little less silky. Use the lower amount of sugar for a sharp taste; use the higher amount for a sweeter taste. Yields about 1 lb.

125 g/4 oz butter
175-225 g/6-8 oz sugar
2 large lemons, rind and juice
2 large eggs, beaten

Put butter, sugar, lemon rind ad half of the strained juice into a 2.75 litre/4 pint bowl.

Cook uncovered on full power for 3 min. Stir well until butter is melted and sugar dissolved.

Add remainder of strained lemon juice and beaten eggs. Continue cooking uncovered for 5 min or until mixture has thickened enough to coat the back of a spoon. Check and stir every minute.

Pour into small, heated jam jars. Cover surface immediately with a waxed paper disc. Cover with a clean cloth until quite cold, and then fasten on the jam pot covers. Store in refrigerator if possible and use within 6 weeks.

Note: The curd tends to thicken more as it cools in the jars. If for some reason it does not, return mixture to bowl and beat in another egg yolk. Continue to cook on full power, stirring each minute as before.

MARMALADE
James Barlow, Rothwell, Leeds

8 Seville oranges
2 sweet oranges
1 lemon
4 pints water
4 lb sugar

Wash all fruits preferably scrubbing to remove any blemishes or dead insects on the skin. Cut fruit into segments and remove all pips and cores and put these in a muslin bag. Put all peel and fleshy part of fruit through a mincer then place it in a bowl, covering with the water.

Having secured the muslin bag containing the pips, etc., place in the bowl of water with the peel, etc. and leave overnight. Next day, place in a preserving pan and simmer for 1½ to 2½ hours. The peel should squash easily between thumb and forefinger. Remove bag, squeeze our juice into a saucer and stand for a while. If it sets, it is ready and may be poured in jars.

PLUM JAM
Anne Garrison, ex-Halifax, now Reading, Berkshire

"My mother made raspberry and gooseberry jams but she bottled plums rather than making them into jam. We also collected blackberries to make jam; my aunts also made strawberry jams and blackcurrant jam because they grew them. Usually apple and bramble are in the same jam as it makes the brambles go further!"

2 kg/4 lb) plums
259 ml (8 fl oz) water
1½ kg (3 lbs) granulated sugar

Remove the stones from the plums and put the fruit into a large saucepan with the water. Simmer until the plums are tender.

Add the sugar and stir until it has dissolved. Boil rapidly for about 10 to 20 minutes until the setting point is reached.

Remove from the heat and leave for 10 minutes. Ladle into hot sterilized jars, label and seal.

You may wish to add a Tbsp of grated root ginger when adding the sugar.

VICTORIAN APPLE JAM
Sherry

"This is a very old, 19th century recipe, which I found reproduced in a book called Seven Hundred Years of English Cooking. It's definitely very old. It does not say how much sugar, if any, to add."

Pour into a clean earthen pot two quarts of spring water; and throw into it as quickly as they can be pared, quartered and weighed, four pounds of nonesuches, pear mains, Ripstone pippins, or any other good boiling apples of fine flavour. When they are done, stew them gently until they are well broken, but not reduced quite to pulp.

Turn them into a jelly bag, or strain the juice from them without pressure through a closely woven cloth, which should be gathered over the fruit, and tied, and suspended above a deep pan until the juice ceases to drop from it; this, if not very clear, must be rendered so, before it is used for syrup or jelly, but for all other purposes once straining, it will be sufficient.

QUINCES

are prepared in the same way, and with the same proportions of fruit and water, but they must not be too long boiled, or the juice will become red. We have found it answers well to have them simmered until they are perfectly tender and then to leave them with their liquor in a bowl until the following day, when the juice will be rich and clear.

They should be thrown into the water very quickly after they are pared and weighed, as the air will soon discolour them. The juice will form a jelly much more easily if the cores and pips be left in the fruit.

NOTES

PUDDINGS AND DESSERTS

BAKED SUET PUDDING
See Suet Puddings

Sweet suet puddings are made much the same way as savoury suet puddings. You can roll the pastry out, spread jam on it and steam it.

BAKEWELL PUDDING

¼ lb butter
2 egg yolks
¼ lb sugar
almond flavouring

Cream butter and sugar, add egg yolks and beat thoroughly.

Put into a jar in a pan of water and let boil until it is as thick as cream. When nearly cold, add flavouring. Line saucers with a rich pastry spread with a layer of raspberry jam and cover with the mixture.
Bake in a quick over (425°F) until lightly brown on top.

BATTER PUDDING WITH APPLES
Christina Flanigan, California

Apples may be substituted for whatever fruit strikes your fancy or have on hand. Soft fruits are better cooked in a basin.

BATTER
8 oz plain flour
2 eggs
1 pint milk
1 Tbsp fat or lard
¼ tsp salt

Sift flour and salt into a basin. Make a well in the centre of the flour and break the eggs into this. Add about a gill (half) of the milk, stir gradually working the flour down from the sides and adding more milk as required to make a stiff batter.

Beat well for about 5 min. Add rest of the milk. Cover and leave to stand for at least 30 min.

APPLE FILLING
1 lb apples
2 oz sugar
¼ tsp cinnamon or grated lemon rind
¼ oz butter

Core, peel and slice the apples thinly. Sprinkle with the sugar and cinnamon or lemon rind. Spread them over a well-greased Yorkshire pudding tin.

Pour the batter over and flake the butter on top.

Bake in a hot (425°F) oven until brown, about 20-25 min.

BREAD PUDDING

8 oz stale bread (French is best)
4 oz currants or raisins or sultanas
2 oz brown sugar
2 oz finely chopped suet or butter
generous ½ tsp mixed spice
1 egg
a little milk

Break hard bread into small pieces; soak in cold water at least ½ hour; then strain and squeeze as dry as possible. Put into a basin and beat out the lumps with a fork. Add the dried fruit, sugar, suet, peel and mixed spice and mix well. Add the egg and enough milk to enable the mixture to drop easily from a spoon. Put into an 8" greased tin. Bake at 335ºF for about an hour. Dredge with sugar and serve with custard or vanilla sauce.

BREAD & BUTTER PUDDING (1)
Carol

Slices of bread and butter
2 oz sugar
3 eggs
1½ pints milk
¼ lb currants or sultana raisins
grated nutmeg or lemon

Thickly butter slices of bread and put a layer on the bottom of a pie dish. Sprinkle a few currents or raisins over, lay more slices of bread and butter and sprinkle again and repeat until the dish is filled.

Boil the milk, and pour it hot on to the well beaten eggs. Add to this the sugar and spice, then pour over the bread and butter in the dish. Bake slowly for 1 hour. Serves 8.

BREAD & BUTTER PUDDING (2)
James Barlow, Rothwell, Leeds

2 eggs
1 pint milk
vanilla flavouring or lemon essence
fruit (sultanas, etc.)
sugar

Beat eggs in milk and add vanilla flavouring or lemon essence.

Butter a pie dish. Cut 3 slices of bread and remove crust, butter and cut into fingers. Put a layer of bread in pie dish, butter side up.

Sprinkle fruit and sugar on bread, add another layer of bread and butter. Add more fruit, sugar and bread as required. Pour over the milk, egg and flavouring and leave to soak one hour. Bake in slow over for 1 hour.

DEB'S SUET PUDDING (1)
Susan Waters, Virginia

"The recipes I ha are from Ohio early in the 20th century. When that area was established (1830s, 1840s) it was called The English Settlement (they were from Yorkshire). When this cookbook was collected (they are recipes from people in the area) the town was a mix of English, Irish, Scots and German. This recipe is probably English/Yorkshire. Apparently they knew how to cook it because cooking instructions were not included. I suspect it must be a steamed pudding."

3 cups sugar
1 cup molasses
2 cups sugar
2 cups sour milk
3 cups soda
cinnamon, cloves, allspice

NUTMEAT
½ lb currants
½ lb raisins
flour

SAUCE FOR THE PUDDING
1 ½ cups sugar
1 pint water
1 Tbsp corn starch or flour
butter the size of an egg
nutmeg

DELAWARE PUDDING (1)
Jean Spence, South Australia

"My mum used to make a sweet where she sandwiched suet pastry and mixed fruit alternately in a bowl then steamed it. This is what I think she called it."

FRUIT "STEAK & PUDDING"
Tana Willis Johnson, Gloucestershire

"My granny used to make a fruit version of the Steak and Kidney Pudding, with sugar in the pastry. She filled the basin with plums and sugar or apples and brown sugar. Not too much water as the fruit made its own juice. She served it with custard."

FRUIT PUDDING
Tana Willis Johnson, Gloucestershire

"Proper English – Traditional as a Christmas pudding. Reet proppa fruit Pud we' traditional ingredients – takes hours to prepare and at least 7 hours to cook. Enjoy the experience! This should make you three puddings. In 1947 this cost 17 shillings and sixpence to make (I know 'cos me mother wrote it down). It's probably more like 17 quid now! My advice is not to cook this on the day you plan to serve it. Do it at least a couple of weeks before. The day you plan to serve, it just requires an hour's cooking time using the same method. These puddings will last a year if properly sealed in the basin and kept somewhere cool. You could put them in the freezer although I have never tried this.

DO NOT UNDER ANY CIRCUMSTANCES MICROWAVE THIS GLORIOUS PUD!"

1½ lb shredded suet *(shows how old this recipe is, you can't get it anymore. Use packed suet)*
8oz stoned and halved plums
8oz chopped mixed peel
1 lb seedless raisins *(get those wonderful Aussie kind – the best you can afford)*
1 lb sultanas
1 lb currants
4oz chopped walnuts
4 oz ground almonds
1 lb soft dark brown sugar
12 oz sifted flour
4 oz fresh breadcrumbs

finely grated peel of 2 oranges and 1 lemon
1 tsp freshly grated nutmeg
½ tsp cinnamon
½ tsp allspice´
2 tsp salt
8 eggs
½ pint milk
¼ pint Brandy

Wash all the fruit thoroughly – soak it all in a large bowl while you are sorting out all the other ingredients. Mix all the dry ingredients in a very large bowl and add the washed fruit.

Beat the eggs and add them and the milk and Brandy. Mix thoroughly – this should take at least 15 min and everyone in the house must have a go – this is vital to the whole process – it just won't come out right if they don't. Everyone must then have a teaspoon of the mixture to see if there's enough Brandy in it. If there isn't, you know what do!

Leave it in a cool place for 12 hours. Put the mixture into either muslin bags or greased pudding basins. If pudding basins are used they should be securely covered with foil and tied very tightly under the rim.

Get the largest pot you can find and half fill with boiling water. Gently place the pudding in the pan and bring to the boil, turn down the heat to a continuous but gentle bubble and steam for 7 hours.

GOLDEN PUDDING
Christina Flanigan, California

4 oz marmalade
4 oz plain flour
4 oz breadcrumbs
3 oz finely chopped suet
2 oz caster sugar

1 rounded tsp baking powder
2 eggs
pinch of salt
1 gill (½ cup) of milk

Grease a 2 pint pudding basin. Spread 2 oz marmalade over the base.

Mix together flour, breadcrumbs, suet, sugar, baking powder and salt.

Beat together the eggs, remaining 2oz marmalade and a little of the milk. Stir this mixture into the dry ingredients and add milk as required to mix to a dropping consistency.

Put the mixture into a basin, cover with greased paper and steam for 1½ hours. Serve with marmalade sauce.

LEMON SWEET
Susan Cook, Westbank, B.C.

¼ pint double cream
6 oz condensed milk
2 large lemons

Mix cream, condensed milk and grated lemon rind and beat in food mixer until thick.

Gradually add juice of lemons. Pour on a crumb base. Place in freezer until firm. Thaw for at least ½ hour before serving.

MRS. BARNES' CARROT PUDDING

2 cups grated carrots
2 tsp baking powder
1 cup grated suet
½ tsp cinnamon
½ cup sugar
½ tsp cloves
¾ cup sifted flour
2 oz raisins
1 tsp salt
2 oz currents

½ cup breadcrumbs
½ cup chopped pecans
1 cup mixed candied fruits and cherries

Sift all dry ingredients and add to the rest. But into buttered mould. Steam 3½ hours.

NORTHAMPTONSHIRE PUDDING
Beverley Ramsden, Renfrew, Ontario

2 oz butter
2 eggs
4 oz flour
1 Tbsp raspberry jam
3 oz sugar

Cream the butter and sugar. Let stand for a5 min, then add flour and eggs, alternately. Lastly, mix in jam. Steam for 2 hours.

SWEET SUET PUDDINGS

ROLY POLY BREAD PUDDINGS

Roly Poly is a favourite steamed Yorkshire suet pudding. You can substitute margarine but for those who want to be accurate, ask your butcher or the fat from around the kidney. Suet is used because it has a high melting point, consequently it leaves lovely airy holes throughout the pudding. You can get almost the same effect with butter or margarine – freeze it first then quickly put it through your food processor or a grating disk or grate it on a cheese grater. Do it very quickly and at the last minute so the fat stays frozen as long as possible.

There are several favourite steamed puddings, all of which involve basins and white boiling cloths: the pudding is boiled for a couple of hours. It's okay, you can do some of them in the microwave now! First is the traditional recipe then the microwave one.

ROLY POLY PUDDING (1)

12 oz all purpose flour
2 rounded tsp baking powder
6 oz finely chopped suet
pinch of salt
water to mix
jam

Sift the flour and baking powder, add the suet and salt. Mix with sufficient water to make a soft but firm dough.

Roll it into a rectangle about ¼ in thick. Spread with jam almost to the edge. Damp the edges and roll up lightly. Seal the edges.

Wrap the pudding in a scalded well floured cloth; tie up the ends.

Put into fast boiling water. Simmer for 2 to 2½ hours. 6 helpings.

ROLY POLY PUDDING (2)
Carol

1 lb suet paste
jam or treacle

Make 1lb of good suet paste and roll it out to a quarter of an inch in thickness.

Spread it evenly over with any kind of jam or with treacle. Wet the paste and press it firmly together at the ends.

Fold a well-buttered cloth round, tie it at the ends, and tightly pin it in the centre. Boil the pudding for 1½ hours and when cooked, remove the cloth carefully.

A nice sweet sauce can be poured over and around the poly, and if liked, the top can be sprinkled with caster sugar and shredded pistachio nuts.

MICROWAVE ROLY POLY

"I've got several microwave pudding recipes but not one for roly poly. I'm going to guess, using the other recipes as a guide, that you could do roly poly in the microwave but you do have to put it in a suitably sized microwave-safe dish which fits as closely as possible the contours of the pudding. A glass loaf pan might do."

Grease the dish, put the pudding into it, and cover loosely with plastic wrap, pleated to allow for any rising, and pierced to let steam escape.

Cook on high for 10 mins, giving a half-turn half-way through. Leave to stand a few minutes before turning out.

PUZZLE PUDDING
James Barlow
From the Sowerby Parish Church Cookbook

5 Tbsp flour
1 cup milk
2 Tbsp sugar
1 tsp bicarbonate of soda
4 Tbsp suet
3 Tbsp jam
pinch of salt

Mix dry ingredients together, except the soda. Bring milk to boil, add jam and soda to milk, mix well pour over dry ingredients and mix. Steam for 2½ hours. Serve with white sauce.

SWEET DUMPLINGS
Jean Spence, South Australia

Follow the recipe for suet pastry dumplings. Cover with golden syrup and bake until done.

SULTANA PUDDING
Christine Flanigan, California

4 oz butter
1 heaping tsp baking powder
8 oz plain flour
pinch of salt
4 oz caster sugar
4 oz sultanas
2 eggs
few drops vanilla essence
milk to mix

Grease a 2 pint bowl. Clean sultanas. Rub fat into the sifted flour, salt and baking powder. Add the sugar and fruit.

Mix with beaten egg, milk and vanilla essence to a soft dropping consistency. Put the mixture into the basin and cover.

Steam for 1½ - 2 hours. – Turn out, dredge with sugar and serve with custard or lemon sauce.

A CHEAP TRIFLE
Martyn Gleaden, Wath-Upon-Dearne
From a 1900 notebook by Mary Duckett.

3 penny sponge buns
¼ pint milk
2 Tbsp jam
1 Tbsp caster sugar
2 eggs separated
3 drops flavouring

Cut the sponge buns into pieces and place them in a glass dish. Spread them with jam. Make a custard of the yolks, milk, essence and half the sugar.

Pour over the cakes and allow to soak. About a quart of an hour later, mix the second half of the sugar with the stiffly whipped egg whites and pile on top.

TRIFLE
Denise Oyston, Huddersfield

"This is how my mum has always made it and it is my all-time favourite. My sister makes Black Forest trifle, using a chocolate Swiss roll filled with black cherry jam, stoned black cherries, a cherry liqueur and chocolate custard. Another favourite is to substitute Drambuie for the Sherry."

1 large glass fruit bowl to make it in.
½ packet trifle sponges or a stale
    Swiss roll
1 packet strawberry jelly mix
Some fruit, either strawberries or
    raspberries, tinned or fresh
1 pint cooled custard
½ pint whipped cream
1 glass Cream Sherry
some strawberry or raspberry jam

Split the trifle sponges and spread with jam. Cut in quarters lengthwise, and place in bowl. Sprinkle sherry over top of sponges. Make up jelly with juice from fruit and water per packet instructions. Arrange fruit over sponges.

Pour jelly over fruit and sponges and put in fridge until set. Pour custard over jelly. Top with fresh whipped cream and decorate as you like.

TRADITIONAL ENGLISH TRIFLE
Cynthia Peat, Toronto

1 jelly roll or sponge spread with jam
¼ to ½ cup Sherry
7 oz whipping cream whipped stiff
14oz English custard cooled

Dip cut cake pieces in Sherry, layer with custard and stiffly whipped cream. Garnish with glacé cherries.

ROSEWATER
Conrad Plowman, Knaresborough

WHERE WOULD YOU BUY ROSEWATER?

You can buy rosewater quite easily in the UK. It is sold in some supermarkets and also health food/vegetarian shops as a food flavouring. You might also find it in the equivalent of our chemist shop – drugstore or whatever, sold as a perfumed additive to bath water, as a skin cleanser, or as a basis for what is described on the bottle as 'floral waters'. However, if it is not sold for culinary purposes, check the ingredients – it should have nothing but water, flavouring and a preservative such as isopropanol.

HOW TO MAKE IT

You can make this in the early summer by picking about 50g rose petals from a fragrant variety just as the buds are opening, covering with water, standing overnight, and straining. However the results are just as good with rosewater from a health food shop, chemist, etc. If you prefer, you can add a handful of currants to the mix, but this wasn't in the original recipe!

SAVOURIES

REGARDING BRAWN

Yorkshire people were very frugal and you can tell from their recipes that many of them knew how to care for families on very limited budgets. Brawn sounds very much like HEADCHEESE that can be bought in Canada as both are made using similar methods and ingredients.
June Ridsdale

Brawn, which correctly means a fleshy muscle, was originally made from a pig's head and trotters. In the Middle Ages, brawns were made from boars' heads and frequently used as centrepieces, heavily decorated with piped creams, glazes and gilding.

During the following centuries, other types of meat were used for brawns. In Wales and North England, cow heel brawn, sometimes with tripe, was a popular dish ad used to be sold from market stalls. The Tunbridge Brawn, made with pig's head, trotters and ears, was particularly heavily spices and more solid in texture than ordinary brawn.

Sheep or calf's head may also be used for brawns, the trotters being replaced by diced bacon in a sheep head brawn and omitted completely in a calf head brawn.
Anne Garrison

BACON DUFF
Tana Willis Johnson, Gloucestershire
A version of suet dumplings

6 slices of lean smoked bacon cut into squares, fat removed
1 leek, 1 carrot, 1 onion
1 cup chopped celery
parsley, thyme, pepper (no salt, the bacon is enough)
some stock

Melt a little butter in a large frying pan (heat fairly fierce). Peel and slice the carrots and add to the pan. While they're cooking, slice the other vegetables and add as they're done.

Put the rest of the ingredients and bring to boil not too much moisture – just enough to be able to see it.

Line the pot with the suet, add the bacon mixture, put top on and boil for an hour. Lovely served with steamed savoy cabbage and mashed potatoes. Serves 4.

BRAINS ON TOAST
Joy Ellis, born Leeds, now Somerset

Take 3 sheep's or lamb's brains, soak in lightly salted water, remove any membranes. Wash thoroughly, but gently. Tie in a muslin bag.

Bring a pan of water to the boiling point and salt add brains, lower heat and simmer gently for 15 min.

Drain and remove from muslin and chop, adding a chopped hard boiled egg. Melt 25 g/2 oz butter in a pan, add brains and egg, heat through, season to taste and add some parsley.

Serve on hot buttered toast.

BRAINS - FRIED
Magdalena Gorrell Guimaraens

Soak and clean brains as before and poach lightly in salted water. Drain, cool and slice lengthwise.

Dip in beaten egg and dredge in breadcrumbs. Fry in butter until golden. Sprinkle with a few drops of lemon juice and serve, garnished with parsley.

BRAWN (1)
Anne Garrison, ex-Harrogate now Reading, Berkshire

1 pig's head
2 pig's trotters
12 peppercorns
1-2 blades mace
1 bay leaf
4 cloves
spring each: parsley, thyme, sage
salt and pepper
6 oz roughly chopped onions
2 hardboiled eggs

Split the head in half, remove the brains and clean the nostrils and teeth by brushing with salt. Rinse, blanch and refresh the head. Soak the head in brine for 3-5 days, using 2 oz salt to 1 pint water.

Clean the head and trotters thoroughly cover with cold water and bring to the boil.

Tie the peppercorns, mace, bay leaf, cloves and herbs in muslin and add to the pan with salt and pepper. Simmer, covered until tender, after about 4 hours.

Lift out the head and trotters, remove the tongue and slice. Remove all the meat from the bones and cut into dice. Place the bones in a pan with 2 pints of the cooking liquid, the onions and seasoning and simmer for 1 hour. Strain stock and reduce to 1 pint.

Wet a mould and line with slices of tongue and hardboiled eggs; fill the mould with diced meat. Pour the reduced stock into the mould and leave to cool and set.

When col, put a weight over the mould and leave in a cold place for about 24 hours. To serve, turn out from the mould, cut into slices and accompany with Oxford Brawn Sauce.

BRAWN (2)
Susan Cook, Westbank, B.C.

½ a pig's head
1 lb beef (ox tail, shirt or skirt)
12 peppercorns tied in muslin
Powdered mace or nutmeg
1 tsp chopped parsley
½ tsp thyme
salt and pepper to taste

Wash head well in cold water and drain. Wipe beef with a damp cloth. Put into a pan or casserole, add seasonings and herbs. Cover with cold water. Bring to the boil and simmer for 4 hours.

Cool, lift the meat into a large dish, remove the bones, chop the meat into small pieces with a sharp knife, return meat to the pan, bring to a boil and stir well.

Pot up into pudding dishes or small moulds. Leave to set in a cool place,

BRAWN (3) (CHICKEN)
Anne Garrison, ex-Harrogate now Reading, Berkshire

3½ lb boiling fowl or chicken
2 pig's trotters
salt and pepper
mixed herbs
Scrumpy or dry bottled cider
2 hardboiled eggs

Place the trussed fowl in a pan with the trotters, salt, pepper and mixed herbs.

Cover with cider or water and bring to the boil Remove to the oven – 300°F/Gas Mark 2 – cover and cook for 4 hours.

Strain the stock and leave the chicken and trotters to cool. Strip the meat from the chicken and trotters, chop finely and correct seasonings if necessary. Return the meat to the liquid and heat through.

Line a wetted mould with sliced hardboiled eggs; pour in the meat and stock pressing down well.

Leave to cool, then press under a weight for several hours.

Turn out when set and garnish with sprigs of watercress.

BRAWN (4) (COW HEEL & BEEF)
Janice Wood

½ cow heel
2 bay leaves
350 gr shin beef
cold water, salt and pepper

Cut up the cow heel and beef and put in pan with seasoning and enough water to just cover the meat.

Simmer for 1 hour or until meat is tender. Put beef and cow heel through mincer. Return to liquid.

Test for seasoning and pour into moulds to set.

BRAWN (5) (KANGAROO TAIL AND PIG'S HEAD)
Karen Smith, Australia

"My mother, a Yorkshire lass, used to make brawn when I was young, but stopped making it later on. - I think when life got easier financially for the family. My mother-in-law used to make it for my father-in-law who loved it. It is, as you can see, fairly economic, although a bit gory by the looks of it. By the way, a dessertspoon is a different measure in Canada and Australia. I think yours is the equivalent of what we call a tablespoon."

1 kangaroo tail
Mixed herbs
1 blade mace
pepper and salt
½ small pig's head

Cut up or joint the kangaroo tail and put it with the pig's head and other ingredients on to boil. Boil until the meat falls off the bones. Then take out all the bones, pour the mixture into shallow dishes, and let stand until set It needs cool weather or an ice chest.

Failing pig's head, I use belly pieces or bacon, half fat – half lean.

BRAWN (6) (OX CHEEK)
Karen Smith, Australia

2 ox cheeks
1 Tbsp salt
1 tsp pepper
½ tsp mace
a little grated nutmeg
allspice

Soak the cheeks in salt and water for an hour or more, and put on to stew gently until quite tender. Add salt and other seasonings.

Take the meat out when well cooked and break up with a fork. Put back into the liquid and mix well.

Pour into a basin previously rinsed with cold water and put aside until set. Turn out and garnish with parsley,

BRAWN (7) (PIG'S HEAD AND FEET)
Karen Smith, Australia

½ pig's head
2 pig's feet
1 lb shin of beef
Allspice

Remove eyes from head and chop the head and feet well. Put head, feet and beef all together in a saucepan and just cover with water. Bring to the boil and continue boiling slowly until meat will fall from bones.

Then take out and remove all bone and gristle. Put in a basin and season well.

Boil liquid down to about half the quantity and pour over the meat. Leave until quite cold and set.

Scrape off any fat that ay have risen to the top then turn out.

BRAWN (8a) (PORK)
Janice Wood

Pig's head weighing about 3 Kg
700g lean beef
6 ml salt
5 ml pepper
Pinch of powdered cloves
1 onion
Pinch of powdered mace

Clean the head well and soak in water for 2 hours. Place in saucepan with the rest of the ingredients, almost cover with cold water and bring to a boil, cooking for about 3 hours or until tender.

Separate the bones and the flesh from the head. Put the bones back into the liquid and boil quickly until reduced so that it will form a jelly when cold. Chop the meat roughly, working quickly to prevent the fat settling in Place in a wet mould basin or cake tin.

Strain some of the hot liquid and pour over. Leave until quite cold and turn out when set.

BRAWN (8b) (PORK)
Mabel Jowsey, New Zealand

"My mother used to make bawn every time we killed a pig. She must have known the recipe off by heart – there were no cookery books at our house."

Essentially the same recipe as before except Mabel uses a 6 lb pig's head and ½ lbs of lean beef. Mabel also recommends using the liquid in which the meat was cooked as an excellent stock for soup, particularly with the addition of vegetables. The fat, after skimming off and clarifying, is a good substitute for lard.

BRAWN (8c) (PORK)
Joy Ellis, born Leeds, now Somerset

Half a pig's head, with eyes, hair and snout removed. Chop into three pieces. Cut 400 g of shin of beef on the bone, in half, crossways. Remove brains and tongue from head. (Use for another dish.)

Scald and clean the head and then soak in salted water for 2 hours, changing the water 3 or 4 times.

Put all the meats in a pan with onions, carrots, mace, peppercorns and bouquet garni. Cover with cold water. Heat to boiling and skim, cover, reduce heat and simmer for 2-3 hours until tender.

Take meat out of stock and drain thoroughly. Reserve stock. Remove all meat from bones, trimming off skin and fat and dice finely. Return bones to stock and bring to boil and boil rapidly, uncovered, to reduce by half.

Put meats in a wetted mould or cake tin. Pour enough stock over meat to just cover it. Stir gently to distribute meat evenly, allow to cool.

Cover and leave in fridge to set. Turn out and serve. This can also be used for Boiled Pig's Head without the stock jelly and leaving to set.

BRAWN (9) (SHEEP'S HEAD)
Karen Smith, Australia

1 sheep's head
mixed spice
1 dessertspoon gelatine
Cayenne pepper
salt
1 pint water

Simmer sheep's head in about 1 pint water for 2 hours, or until the meat leaves the bone.

Cut into small pieces and season to taste with spice, cayenne and salt. Put into a pie-dish or basin, add the liquid and stand in a cool place to set.

In hot weather, it is advisable to add the gelatine and leave overnight.

MUSHY PEAS

Gary Stockdill

"I was in Bradford market and sampled the delights of 'Pie Tom's, this is a wonderful little cafe that sells nowt but pork pies, mushy peas (mint sauce optional) and black pudding. I asked the proprietress for the recipe, and she told me it was simply dried marrowfat peas (these are rock hard when purchased) left to steep (soak) in a bowl of water containing a few teaspoons of bicarbonate of soda, for 12 hours or more (she steeped hers for 24 hours)."

Ian W. Wright

"The place to find real mushy peas is the little cafe upstairs in Barnsley Market! I assume it is still there as it's a while since my last pilgrimage and there are always those who would spoil our world, but until you have been there and enjoyed a pint bowl of mushy peas with a hot pork pie slapped on the top and washed it all down with a pint mug of steaming tea – all crockery being of the 'best' pottery with broad blue rings round it – you've never lived!"

PEASE PUDDING
Dawn Gitlin

"Pease Pudding was a staple in my childhood. I remember that 60 years or so ago you could buy it steaming hot from a stall in Leeds Market. Lovely on a cold winter day."

225 gr split peas (dried peas), washed and soaked overnight
1 medium onion
1 ham bone or some bacon scraps
25 gr butter
1 egg beaten
salt and pepper to taste

Tie the peas loosely in a cloth, place in a saucepan with the onion, ham bone or bacon scraps and enough boiling water to cover. Bring to the boil and cook for 2-3 hours until soft.

Lift out the bag of peas, sieve then add butter, egg and seasoning. Mix well.

Tie up tightly in a floured cloth and boil for another 30 minutes.

PICKLED EGGS
Magdalena Gorrell Guimaraens
Northern Portugal

Hard boil 4 eggs, peel and arrange in a preserve jar. Peel some small onions and garlic cloves and boil them with salt and peppercorns in sufficient vinegar to cover eggs. Close the jars and store for four days before serving. Keep refrigerated after opening.

SEASONED PUDDING
Eileen Morgan

6-8 slices bread
3 medium onions, chopped
1 egg
1 cup Quaker oats
1 Tbsp flour
sage, salt and pepper to taste

Preheat oven to 400°F. Pour boiling water over bread, soak and then drain well. Boil onions until tender, drain well.

Mash bread and onions together. Add egg and mix well. Add all other ingredients and mix.

Put mixture into a baking dish and drizzle dripping from pork roast over top. Bake 40-50 min.

Slice, serve with lots of gravy and enjoy! Serves 8.

SUET IS THE FAT SURROUNDING THE KIDNEYS IN MEAT

SUET PASTRY AND DUMPLINGS FOR STEWS
Jean Spence, South Australia

"I grate the suet up and mix about 50% to flour, i.e., 1 cup suet to 1 cup flour.

Once you have made your pastry you can choose which way to go – savoury or sweet.

Savoury is usually referred to as 'dumplings' and those are made into small balls dropped into a stew and boiled for about 20 minutes before serving the stew.

Steak and Kidney Pie uses suet pastry and steams this. Prepared, bought suet is not as good."

SAVOURY SUET PUDDING
Harry Sayer, Ambleside

"I seem to remember my wife baking these on a tray which suggests a drier mix."

2 medium sized onions
½ lb fine breadcrumbs
2 oz suet
seasoning
1 tsp each thyme, sage, marjoram
1 egg
a little milk

Partly boil onions and chop finely. Add to all other dry ingredients and ix with beaten egg and milk. Pour into a well greased dish and bake in a moderate over (350-375°F) for approximately 45 minutes.

SUET DUMPLINGS
Tana Willis Johnson, Gloucestershire

"Never be tempted to put more suet in! Savoury versions are nice with some fresh parsley chopped into the mixture."

2 oz self-raising flour to 1 oz of shredded suet
pinch of salt

Mix the dry ingredients. The tricky bit is adding the water: take to the tap and turn on and off very quickly, mix in well. The mixture should still be very crumbly. Do the same again and ix in well, The perfect consistency is when it's very difficult to mix and there is a residue of flour and no excess moisture to soak it up.

Baking gives a nice crispy outer crust. The mix can be either shaped into balls, put on a tray and baked in a high oven (+200°C) for about 40 minutes, or into a casserole/stew (same temperature and time).

Float the mixture in one flat round piece on the top of a stew or as a lining in a pudding pot – not too thick and not to the top as it will all expand a great deal, leaving about an inch spare at the top.

Seal the top with greaseproof paper, kitchen foil or the pot lid and boil for an hour, It's always best to cook the filling first particularly if it's meat.

YORKSHIRE SAVOURY PUDDING
Susan Cook, Westbank, B.C

1 lb diced bread
60 oz grated beef suet
½ pint cold milk
2 eggs
1 lb onions
1 tsp mixed herbs – no sage
1 level tsp salt ½ tsp pepper

Soak the diced bread in milk overnight. Parboil the onions, strain and cut into small pieces. Add to the soaked bread together with the grated sugar, well beaten eggs and mixed herbs. Add the seasonings and beat well. Spread into a greased baking tin and cook in a moderate oven for 30-40 mins. Cut into squares and serve with roast meat and gravy.

NOTES

SOUP

CARROTT AND LEEK SOUP
Shirley Taylor-Dawes, ex-Harrogate now Northern Spain

4 large leeks trimmed of almost all the green stalk
1 lb carrots peeled and sliced finely
2 oz butter
4 cups stock
½ cup single cream
salt to taste
freshly grated black pepper to taste
grated hard Cheddar Cheese

Wash leeks and shred into thin strips. Melt butter in a large saucepan and add vegetables. Cook gently, covered, until the leeks become transparent

Stir in hot stock and simmer over low heat for 1 – 1 ½ hours. Cook and pass through sieve or blender

Return to pan, bring to a boil and turn off the heat. Add cream, serve immediately and sprinkle with grated cheese.

CREAM OF CHICKEN SOUP
Susan Cook, Westbank, B.C.

Carcase of chicken
1 onion
1½ pints water
½ oz rice flour
1 egg yolk
½ cup cream
seasoning to taste
little chopped parsley

Simmer carcase with onion and water for 1 hour. Strain and thicken with blended rice flour. Boil up soup, add seasonings and pour over yolk and cream.

HOMEMADE CHICKEN SOUP
Jill, California

"My mother's general recipe involved boiling up the chicken bones to get some good stock, then picking off the tiny scrapings of meat left on the bones. To the broth and meat she added carrots and celery.

Some households used onion too, but my father would have never forgiven onions in the house. A pinch of mixed herbs and handful of pearl barley finished the mix and the soup was left to simmer for hours.

LETTUCE OR CABBAGE SOUP
Magdalena Gorrell Guimaraens
Traditional family recipe

1 head of lettuce
1 potato
1 onion
3 cups chicken stock
1 Tbsp butter
salt and pepper to taste

Shred the lettuce and set aside. Chop onion very fine and potato into small cubes. Melt butter in pan and add onion. Cook until transparent. Add potato and stock and bring to boil. Simmer for 15 mins, add lettuce and serve immediately. You can use dark green cabbage leaves instead.

COW HEEL SOUP
Joy Ellis, born Leeds, now Somerset

1 cow heel
1½ litre water
1 medium onion
1 large carrot
1 stick celery
bouquet garni
salt and pepper to taste
25 gr fine tapioca or sago
1 Tbsp lemon juice
pinch grated nutmeg
3 Tbsp chopped parsley

Scrape and clean cow heel. Put in a deep pan, cover with water and slowly bring to a boil to blanch, Pour off water and divide into pieces.

Put back into pan with 1½ litre water and bring to a boil.

Meanwhile, prepare vegetables and dice. Add to the pan with the bouquet garni. Cover and simmer for 3½ hours or until tender. Remove the meat, set aside, and strain the soup into a clean pan. Season to taste.

Cut some meat from the bones and chop into small pieces.

Bring soup to the boiling point and sprinkle in tapioca or sago. Cook until the grains are quite clear and soft. Add meat, lemon, nutmeg and parsley.

SUGGESTIONS FOR SOUP
June Ridsdale, Maple Ridge, B.C.

"I do not know if rice is popular in Yorkshire or not, but in Canada our family interchanges rice, orzo, a few dried peas and barley, for different textures. Orzo is actually a pasta product that resembles large rice kernels.

Onions are a must with me. Other fresh veggies that I would toss in (small quantities only) are green beans, corn niblets and peas (if not using dried ones)."

SWEETS, CANDIES & OTHER GOODIES

CHERRY WALNUT DIVINITY
June Hanson, San Diego, California.

3 cups brown sugar
1 cup water
1 cup chopped candied cherries
1 cup chopped walnuts
2 egg whites beaten stiff
1 cup corn or golden syrup
1 tsp vanilla flavouring
1/8 tsp salt

Boil sugar, water, syrup and salt to hard ball stage.

Pour slowly, beating constantly, over stiffly beaten egg whites. Beat until candy begins to stiffen.

Drop by teaspoon on waxed paper or onto a well-buttered pan and cut into squares when cool.

COCONUT ICE
Susan Wragg Reddy, ex-Sheffield, now New Jersey

3 lbs loaf sugar
¾ pint of milk
1 lb desiccated coconut
pink food colouring

Dissolve the sugar in the milk then boil for about 10 min or until the candy thermometer reaches 238°F (114°C).

Remove the pan from the heat and stir in the coconut.

Pour half the mixture into an oiled pan. Add the pink colouring to the remaining mixture and pour this over the white base. Leave to cool and mark into bars when half-set.

DIVINITY
Ann Scott, Bingley, West Yorkshire
From an old 1930's cookbook

2 cups sugar
½ cup corn or golden syrup
1/8 tsp salt
2 egg whites
½ tsp vanilla
1 cup chopped nuts
1/8 tsp cream of tartar
½ cup water

Combine sugar, water, syrup, salt and cream of tartar. Cover and boil 5 mins. Uncover. Wipe sides of pan with a damp cloth. Boil without stirring until it reaches the hard ball stage (245-248°F). Remove from the fire.

Pour slowly, beating constantly, over stiffly beaten egg whites. Continue beating until mixture holds its shape when dropped from a spoon. Add flavouring and nuts.

Drop by teaspoon onto waxed paper or pour into well-buttered pan and cut into squares when cool.

HOMEMADE YORKSHIRE HUMBUGS
Ann Scott, Bingley, West Yorkshire

1 lb brown sugar
1 teacupful of water
essence of peppermint

Boil together but do not stir. When water has evaporated, add a few drops of essence of peppermint and pour mixture on a slab using a knife to prevent it running too thin.

Cut some strips and then cut with sharp buttered scissors.

If the strips are pulled before being cut they will be a lovely amber colour. These are very good for children.

STRAWBERRY DIVINITY FUDGE
Mrs. Hanson, Bradford

2 cups sugar
½ cup water
1 cup strawberry preserve
2 egg whites
¼ tsp cream of tartar

Boil sugar, water and cream of tartar to hard boil stage.

Add fresh strawberries which have been drained as dry as possible. Let come to boil again. Pour slowly, beating constantly, over stiffly beaten egg whites. Beat until thick and fluffy.

Pour into well buttered pan. When firm, cut into squares. Any thick preserves or candied fruit may be used instead of strawberries.

TOFFEE TIPS

Always use a heavy saucepan, preferably cast iron. Make sure that your pot is more than large enough because sugar has a tendency to boil over, especially once you add the baking soda when it will bubble up quite a bit. Aside from the danger of gerring seriously burnt, you will have some mess to clean!

HONEYCOMB or CINDER TOFFEE
(also known as SPONGE CANDY)
Art Rapkin

1 lb granulated sugar
½ pint water
4 Tbsp clear vinegar
3 Tbsp golden syrup
½ tsp baking soda, sifted
12 oz chocolate chips
2 Tbsp vegetable shortening
1 (1oz) square unsweetened baking chocolate

Grease an 8" square tin; set aside. Put sugar, vinegar syrup and water in a heavy or cast iron saucepan. *Very important: use a very large pot to prevent boiling over.*

Heat the mixture over medium heat, not high, stirring with a wooden spoon until the sugar and the syrup have melted/blended well Bring to a boil, cover and boil for 3 min Uncover and continue boiling until your candy thermometer registers 285°F. Remove from the heat.

Add the baking soda, stirring well until the bubbles subside a little.

Pour the candy into the tin and leave until it is just beginning to set. Mark into squares with a buttered knife and leave to set completely. Cut or break into pieces.

OPTIONAL CHOCOLATE COATING

12 oz chocolate chips
2 Tbsp vegetable shortening
1 (1oz) square unsweetened baking chocolate

Combine chocolate chips, shortening and baking chocolate in a 2-quart glass bowl. Microwave on HIGH for 2 minutes.

Using a wooden spoon stir mixture to melt. Dip pieces of Cinder Toffee into the chocolate, covering them completely. Let cool on waxed paper

Wrap individually in waxed paper and store in an airtight container.

PLOT OR BONFIRE TOFFEE
June Hanson, San Diego, California

1 lb brown sugar
4 oz butter
4 oz treacle
1 Tbsp vinegar
1 Tbsp water
1 Tbsp milk

Put everything except vinegar in a saucepan and bring to the boil stirring constantly. Boil gently for 15-20 min, still stirring, until a drop of the mixture becomes brittle when dropped into cold water. Remove from heat and stir in vinegar.

Pour into a well-greased shallow tin. When nearly set, score deeply with a knife into bite-sized squares.

TOM TROT
Susan Cook, Westbank, B.C.

"This dark treacle toffee comes primarily from Swaledale and was a favourite delicacy on Guy Fawkes Night."

½ lb brown sugar
½ lb dark treacle
¼ lb real butter

Put all the ingredients in a pan ad simmer for half an hour. Drop a small quantity in cold water and if it crackles after a short time it is ready.

Pour on to a greased dish and work it with the hands pulling into long lengths and twisting until the toffee is bright and clear.

Break the twists into pieces when cold.

TREACLE TOFFEE (1)

"We would pour the mixture into the tin, let it set, then crack it into pieces with a small hammer. You have to watch for the pointy bits, though!"

1 lb brown sugar
½ lb treacle (molasses)
2 oz butter
2 Tbsp water
1 Tbsp orange juice

Put all ingredients into a saucepan and allow the sugar to dissolve over a low heat. Boil to the 'small crack' degree (290°F) and pour onto a buttered tin.

Mark into squares when partially set and break when firm. Wrap in waxed paper and store in an airtight tin.

TREACLE TOFFEE (2)
Susan Wragg Ready, ex-Sheffield, now New Jersey

Golden syrup can be substituted for the treacle for a milder, less bitter taste.

1½ lb brown sugar
8 oz butter
1 lb treacle
½ pint water
pinch of cream of tartar

Put all ingredients except the cream of tartar into a pan, cover and bring to the boil rapidly. When the toffee boils, add the cream of tarter – dissolved in a little cold water.

Replace the lid, continue boiling for a few minutes longer. Remove the lid, wash down the sides of the pan with a brush dipped in cold water, then boil to 260°F or until a drop of the mixture forms a hard ball in cold water.

When this stage is reached turn off the heat. Pour into oiled tins, leave to cool, and mark with a knife and break into pieces when cool.

SPANISH LIQUORICE
Ann Scott

What is Spanish? Spanish to all Yorkshire folk, is in fact liquorice and Pontefract is the home of liquorice.

When we were small children we could buy thick hard sticks of liquorice from the Chemist. When we got home with them we would put them into a corked bottle full of cold water and shake the bottle. After a while, the water would turn black and we had made or own liquorice pop! Sounds awful – but tasted really good!

Sometimes we would buy a small thin stick of liquorice from the Sweet Shop for half a penny. With this we bought two pennyworth of coloured kali – a soft, sweet powder in various flavours. We would lick our liquorice stick and dip it into the kali and suck it. The kali would last for ages! Your mouth would usually turn a funny coloured shade. It was bliss!

PONTEFRACT or POMFRET CAKES

"These black Yorkshire products are little black lozenges made from liquorice (possibly brought by the Romans) at Pontefract, a town in the southeast of Leeds. Liquorice (Glycyrrhizaglabra) was found to grow very freely at Pontefract (although not in other parts of the country) early on.

Chaucer wrote: "…but first he cheweth greyn and licorys to smellen swete", and from Elizabeth I's reign onwards it was used as a medicine as well as a sweet. It is also said to quench thirst if held in the mouth.

In 1760, a Yorkshire chemist added sugar to the dried roots to make a sweetmeat. The roots of the plant are boiled, mashed and dried then mixed with sugar, treacle, flour, glucose and water until it set solid. They are shaped into cone-shaped lozenges and stamped with an impression of Pontefract Castle."

Extracted by Ann Scott from a very ancient book.

YORKSHIRE PUDDING

*Properly made Yorkshire pudding,
served promptly out of the oven with a good gravy,
is the eighth wonder of the world!*

"A batter pudding traditionally eaten with roast beef. In Yorkshire it is usually served separately before the meal, accompanied by some of the hot beef gravy, but in much the rest of the country the pudding is served with the meat. It may be cooked either in a separate tin or around or under the joint. If preferred the mixture can be made up as small individual puddings or popovers."

In *Good Housekeeping Cookery Encyclopaedia*(1964)

GENERAL TIPS

According to Mrs. Beaton (and who dares argue?), the lightness of Yorkshire pudding batter "depends on the quick formation of steam within the mixture and the quick cooking of the flour. A baked batter therefore requires a hot over (425°F, Gas 7); the temperature can be reduced when the flour is cooked." Other than that, the only caution is that the batter be allowed to stand for 30 minutes. I suspect that "quick formation of steam" might be delayed by the use of ice water.

Mrs. Beaton's USA equivalent, *The Joy of Cooking* insists: "The ingredient must be at room temperature when mixed or they will not puff." Contrarily, the instructions go on to say that the batter be refrigerated when left to stand, but you must bear in mind that American summers are HOT and 30 minutes at room temperature will probably curdle the milk. Here the mixture is beaten again before cooking.

Keith Floyd confides: "The secret of making Yorkshire pudding is to ensure that the oven is very hot, and that the fat in your tin in [just] smoking hot before pouring in the batter." He apparently advocates room temperature for standing time; there is no mention of refrigeration.

We suggest you try these slightly different methods every Sunday until you get it right for you.

MRS. BEATON'S YORKSHIRE PUDDING

Originally published in 1859-61 in monthly supplements. First published as one volume in 1861 entitled: *The Book of Household Management*. The following recipe is from the Enlarged First Edition Facsimile published in the UK in 1982 by Chancellor Press, p. 694.

1 ½ pint milk
6 large Tbsp flour
3 eggs
1 saltspoonful salt

Put the flour into a basin with the salt and stir gradually to this enough milk to make it into a stiff batter.

When this is perfectly smooth, and all the lumps are well rubbed down, add the remainder of the milk and the eggs, which should be well beaten.

Beat the mixture for a few more minutes, and pour it into a shallow tin, which has been previously well rubbed with beef dripping.

Put the pudding into the oven and bake it for an hour, then for another ½ hour; place it under the eat, to catch a little of the gravy that flows from it.

Cut the pudding into small pieces, put them on a hot dish and serve.

FOR MODERN OVENS: Bake at 425ºF until brown (about 20-25 min) then at 375ºF about 10-15 mins.

GRANNY'S YORKSHIRE PUDDING WITH ONIONS
Susan Wragg Reddy, ex-Sheffield, now New Jersey

"Granny knows best, especially when making Yorkshire Puddings.

However, there are some golden rules to follow: you must cook on a high heat first, then turn the oven down; and you mustn't open the oven door at all for the first 20-25 minutes.

And for the most successful results, make your mixture a day in advance and leave it to rest in the fridge, This recipe serves 4."

8 oz plain flour
8 eggs
1 pint milk
2 oz good dripping
salt and freshly ground black pepper

ONION GRAVY
2 white onions, peeled and diced
250 ml (6 fl oz) red wine
400 ml (14 fl oz) fresh beef stock

Place the flour and some seasoning into a bowl. Add the eggs, mixing in with a whisk and then the milk, mixing slowly to prevent lumps forming. At this point, put the bowl in the fridge overnight, covered with some cling film.

Pre-heat the oven to 220ºC/425ºF.

Take four non-stick Yorkshire pudding tins (about 6" in diameter). Put a little dripping in each of the tins, but don't use it all. Put the tins in the oven.

Before you add the mix to the tins, the fat should be smoking hot. As you pour in the mix so that it fills the tins to the top, the mix should seal on the edges.

Working fast, place them back in the oven, close the door and leave it closed for about 20-2 minutes.

Meanwhile, cook the onions in a pan in the remaining dripping about 10 minutes, then add the wine and stock. Reduce until you have a nice thickened mixture, about 10 min.

Turn the oven down to 190°C/375°F/Gas 5 and cook the Yorkshires for a further 10 minutes to set the bottom of the puds thoroughly. Remove from the oven, place on plates and serve the thick onion gravy in the middle... Delicious!

SAVOURY YORKSHIRE PUDDING
Miss Roberts, Bradford

8 oz suet
salt and pepper
8 oz breadcrumbs
1 tsp sage
2 fairly large onions
1 or 2 eggs~
1 Tbsp coarse cornmeal

Chop onions and suet very fine, grate bread, add other dry ingredients and mix together with well-beaten eggs. Bake in well-greased tins for ½ hour.

SEASONED PUDDING
David Hinde, Roscoe, Illinois

"What I have done over the years when doing a pork roast is to make up the usual Yorkshire pud batter (I use 4 eggs, 2 cups of milk and 1 cup of flour) for the standard pud – but for Seasoned put I increase the flour to nearly match the milk quantity – with the extras thrown in, it won't rise as high anyway.) Then I mince onion up about ½ of a small to medium onion and sauté it in the fat I'm going to use for the pud.

Just before the onions become brown, I add "some" sage, rosemary and thyme – about a US tsp each, or what you can cup in the corner of a t' curled up palm of your hand, then dump that lot into the baking tin,

The pan goes into the oven at 425°F until it's hot enough, then the batter gets poured in, and quickly swirled around with a wooden poon, to mix it all together. Pop it back into the oven. Twenty minutes later, turn the oven down to 375°F, give it about 15-20 minutes more, and you're set to serve the pud – before the meat, of course."

YORKSHIRE PUDDING (1)
Audrey, Illinois

"My father came from Leeds and his family always ate the Yorkshire Pudding first, with beef gravy. This was to fill everyone up so that the beef would go further. Believe it or not he lied it with a scattering of currants in it.! To this day I make Yorkshire Pudding with roast beef and my children and my grandchildren love it. We have also convinced the sons-in-law and daughters-in-law to love it also. All my daughters carry on the tradition. Incidentally, I now use skimmed milk and you can't tell the difference."

1 cup flour
2 eggs
1 cup milk
salt

Mix eggs and milk together, beat well. Gradually add egg mixture to flour and salt. Beat well (no lumps). Let stand a while before cooking,

Pre-heat oven to about 450°F. Heat a small amount of shortening in a shallow pan approximately 9" x 13", or individual pans.

When the fat is spluttering, add mixture and put back into the top shelf of the oven. It takes about 20 mins.

"I purchased my pans years ago when back for a visit. It is hard to describe how it should look, but it should have risen around the edges and in the middle and should have browned. It should be eaten as soon as possible I always have to double the recipe."

YORKSHIRE PUDDING (2)
Joan Richie, California

"My father was born and raised in England. His Aunt is pure Yorkshire and her Yorkshire Pudding recipe, a true hand-me-down, is simple and incredible. The roast beef is just a necessary by-product as far as my family is concerned. Plan to double the recipe. This one makes about 12."

1 cup flour
1 cup milk
1 egg
salt to taste – some garlic salt
Bake in muffin (cupcake) tins

Spoon 1 tsp drippings into each muffin. Fill ½ full with batter. Bake 15 min.

Put the Yorkshire in to bake when you take out the roast. By the time it rests and is carved the pudding is ready. They fluff up so nicely.

Serve immediately as they fall although they still taste great. You really need to make a double batch!

YORKSHIRE PUDDING (3)
Roy Smith, Melbourne, Australia

4 oz plain flour (1 US cup all-purpose flour)
1 egg
½ pint of milk & cold water (1¼ US cups
pinch of salt

Heat the oven to 425°F or Gas Mark 7 (220°C). Sieve the flour & salt into a bowl. Make a well in the centre and add the egg. Add half the liquid, a little at a time, mixing with a wooden spoon from the centre outwards and gradually drawing in the flour. Mix until smooth and stir in the remainder of the milk.

Pour 1 tablespoon of the dripping from the meat pan into the Yorkshire pudding tin or shallow fireproof dish and return it to the oven for 2 minutes. When it is really hot pour in the batter and bake in a hot oven for about 40 minutes. If cooking individual puddings (or popovers), cook for about 20-30 minutes.

The Yorkshire Pudding should be a nice golden brown colour, not black!

Serve cut in squares, as an accompaniment to roast beef, etc.

TIPS, CUSTOMS & REMARKS

Standing the batter in a cool place to let it "settle" is essential. And one other essential secret is to beat in a tablespoonful of iced water into the batter just before pouring it into the hot beef fat. This puts sufficient air into the mixture to make it rise and give it a lovely crisp top.
Roy Smith

Most Yorkshire women I know don't measure their ingredients. My Mom always adds iced water and so do I. I use a mixer and iced water and milk and leave the batter to stand for at least half an hour before cooking,
Susan Wragg Reddy

My Grandma used to make an extra batch of Yorkshire Pudding just in case we still had room when we had finished our meal and we would have milk and sugar on them, sometimes jam. I would only eat them with milk and sugar on.

Anonymous

WARTIME TASTIES

Most of these recipes are from a book Compiled by the Women's Volunteer Services for Civil Defence (Barnsley Centre) at the request of the War Emergency Committee for the Mayor of Barnsley's Spitfire Fund December 1940
Contributed by John B. Price, Metairie, Louisiana

CHEAPER THAN BUTTER

Take 4 or 5 large potatoes, add salt to taste and cook them well. When done, strain and let them stand five minutes. Get 2 beef cubes and ¼ lb of margarine and beat these into the warm potatoes till both are dissolved. Turn into a dish and flatten with a knife. It is then ready to spread on your bread and saves butter.

(Submitted by the Deputy Mayoress, Mrs. G. Mason, President, Barnsley WVS, Nov 1939 to Nov 1940.)

CURRANT BREAD

3 lb flour
¼ lb lard
½ lb sugar
1 lb fruit
2 oz yeast
Salt

Mix with warm milk and water. Knead and allow to rise like plain bread.

(Submitted by Mrs. J. Brown, Dodworth Road.)

DATE BREAD

1 cupful sugar
2 cupfuls flour
1 egg
2 oz chopped walnuts
1 lb stoned dates
1 oz margarine
1 tsp bicarbonate of soda

Stone ad cut the dates, sprinkle bicarbonate of soda over them; pour 1 cupful of boiling water over them and leave to cool. Sub the margarine into the flour, add sugar and beaten egg, dates and nuts which have been chopped.

Stir well and put into two well greased tins and let stand for 20 minutes before baking. Bake in a moderate oven for 1 ½ to 2 hours.

(Submitted by Mrs. Cooper)

In Wartime, people showed great ingenuity in planning their meals. Yorkshire women were determined to care for their families, despite all odds.

FAT RASCALS

1 lb flour
½ lb cooking fat
1 oz sugar
¼ lb currants
½ tsp salt
milk and water to mix

Rub the fat into the flour, add currants, sugar and salt. Mix to a firm dough with milk and water. Roll out half inch thick, cut into rough squares, bake in quick oven.

(Submitted by Mrs. Stooke)

FRUITED BROWN BREAD

3½ cupfuls brown flour
1 cupful white flour
1 cupful sugar (or less)
6 oz raisins
1 tsp bicarbonate of soda
4 good Tsp treacle
1 pint of mil (or less)

Mix all dry ingredients together; add treacle, stir well adding milk gradually (do not warm treacle or milk)

Well grease three 2 lb loaf tins, pour in mixture. Bake in moderate oven for 1 hour (Regulo 3). Can be eaten with or without butter.

(Submitted by Mrs. Archer, Hope Street)

FRUITED LOAVES

4 lbs flour
½ lb lard, rubbed in
½ lb sugar
1 lb stoned raisins
1 lb currants
¼ lb mixed peel
1½ oz yeast
2 eggs, well beaten

Mix with warm milk ad proceed as for bread. This makes 4 loaves.

(Anonymous)

GINGER BREAD

3oz butter or margarine
9 oz flour
3 oz fine oatmeal
3 oz sugar
7 ½ oz treacle
1 small tsp baking powder
½ tsp ground ginger
1 egg

Cream butter, add treacle and beat. Beat the egg and add to butter and treacle. Mix dry ingredients and add gradually to butter, etc., and if necessary add a little milk. Bake in a moderate oven.

(Submitted by Mrs. Southwick)

HARVO BREAD

2 cupfuls brown flour
2 cupfuls white flour
2 oz lard
1 cupful sugar
1 tsp bicarbonate of soda
1 cupful dark treacle
½ lb raisins
1½ cupfuls milk

Bake in moderate oven for 2 hours.

(Submitted by Mrs. Squire, Mona Street)

HOT CROSS BUNS

3 oz flour
6 oz sugar
6 oz lard
9 oz mixed fruit
1 tsp salt
1 tsp mixed spice
1 tsp nutmeg

¼ lb lemon peel
¼ lb yeast
1 egg

Rub all together and make a hole, drop in egg (well beaten). Crumble in the yeast and a little sugar. Put to sponge with milk and warm water, knead into a light dough. Leave it half an hour to rise. Make into buns, mark with a cross and bake for 15 to 20 minutes.

(Submitted by Mrs. A. Lofthouse, Queen's Avenue)

MALT BREAD

10 oz flour
1 cupful sugar
1 cupful boiling water
5 oz margarine
2 oz dates
4 oz raisins
2 ¼ tsp baking powder
¼ tsp bicarbonate of soda
2 oz chopped nut

Pour boiling water over the dried fruits, sugar and margarine, in a mixing bowl. Place in the oven and simmer for about 5 minutes. When cold, mix in flour, nuts and rest of dried fruits and baking powder. Bake in moderate oven 1½ hours.

(Submitted by Mrs. Caven)

MAIDS OF HONOUR
Judith Kettlewell

[Submitted by Ellen Rowbothem & Mrs. Wilkinson & Anon., Fagley Bradford. The exact title of the cookbook is unknown as the original cover was lost. Possibly edited by the T&A.]

Mix 1 oz margarine with 2 Tbsp syrup; add 4 Tbsp quick cooking oats and 1 dried egg, reconstituted, 1 tsp baking powder & almond essence to taste. Line patty tins with pastry, putting a little raspberry jam and a teaspoonful of the mixture in each. Bake in a moderate oven.

PLUM LOAF

2½ lb flour
1½ lb sugar
½ lb butter
¼ lard or margarine
1 nutmeg
¼ lb candied peel
1 lb sultanas
1 lb currants
5 or 6 eggs
3 tsp baking powder
½ tsp bicarbonate of soda
½ breakfast cupful golden syrup
milk and water to mix

This makes 4 good-sized loaves.

(Submitted by Miss A. Gibson, Huddersfield Road)

SPICE LOAF

¼ lb stone flour
2 lb sugar
¼ tsp baking powder
1½ lb currants
1½ lb sultanas
¼ lb mixed peel
1 lb lard
1½ lb margarine
4 eggs
½ nutmeg grated~
2 tsp bicarbonate of soda

Mix all ingredients together with a little lukewarm milk until it falls from the spoon. Bake in a moderate over for 2 hours.

(Submitted by Mrs. F. Crosby, Withorpe)

YORKSHIRE PARKIN

6 oz flour
6 oz oatmeal
2 oz lard
4 oz sugar
1 lb dark treacle
1 tsp ground ginger
1 tsp bicarbonate of soda

Mix flour, oatmeal and sugar together, rub in the lard, then add treacle. Mix bicarbonate of soda with warm water. Put into well-greased tin and bake in a moderate oven for ¾ hour.

(Submitted by Miss D. Pierrepont, Lingard Street)

HOT MEAT SALAD

This is a useful way to use leftovers when the family threatens to leave the house if it sees cold meat again.

Cut the meat into slices and lay them in a greased fireproof dish. Pour over them a roux, white or brown. This is flour and butter in equal quantities, melted together, stock, a bunch of fresh herbs, pepper, salt, brought to the thickening stage of boiling.

Next, sprinkle mixed oil and vinegar over, add a layer of breadcrumbs, put the dish in the oven for 20 minutes – and see if the family leaves any for tomorrow! Tomatoes are an excellent addition to the roux.

(Submitted by Mrs. Mellor, Lingard Street)

PEA FRITTERS

1 small packet of dried peas
1 lb mashed potatoes
salt and pepper
small piece butter or margarine

Soak peas overnight. Boil in the usual way. Boil and mash potatoes. Mix both together with a pinch of salt, pepper and butter. When cool, form into balls with floured hands.

Dip into batter made with:
3 heaped Tbsp flour
pinch of salt
pinch bicarbonate of soda
Mix with water to form thick batter.

Fry in deep hot fat till golden brown. Serve hot, with vinegar.

(Submitted by Mrs. Eyre)

SALAD FOR SANDWICH FILLING

"Two large potatoes passed through a kitchen sieve, smoothness and softness to a salad give.

Of mordant mustard add a single spoon. Distrust the condiment that bites too soon, but deem it not, mixer of herbs, a fault to add a double quantity of salt.

Four times the spoon with oil of olive crown and twice with vinegar procured from town. True flavour needs it, and your poet begs.

The pounded yellow of two well boiled eggs. Let onion's atoms lurk within the bowl, and, scarce suspected, animate the whole.

Then lastly, in the flavoured mixture toss a magic spoonful of anchovy sauce. Oh Great and glorious! A herbaceous treat.

'Twould tempt the dying Anchorite to eat. Back to the world he'd turn his weary soul and plunge his fingers in the salad bowl."

(Submitted by Mrs. Andrews, Denby Dale)

RUSSIAN EGG DISH

hard-boiled chopped egg
little minced Parmesan cheese
1 raw egg slightly beaten, with a little milk
salt and pepper

Cook slightly together and place on one half of small pancakes, folding the other side over and pressing the edges slightly together with a spoon.

Sprinkle with Parmesan and place in a fireproof dish. Put in oven for a moment to get thoroughly hot. They should be about the size of jam puffs.

Mushrooms, shrimps, prawns, chopped vegetables, or little bits of chicken may be added to the egg.

(Submitted by the Countess of Wharncliffe)

FISH CAKES

The remains of any cold fish
to each 1 lb allow ½ lb mashed potatoes
1 oz margarine
Breadcrumbs
1 egg
milk, salt and pepper

Heat the margarine in a saucepan. Add the fish, coarsely chopped, potatoes, half of the egg, salt and pepper and sufficient milk to moisten thoroughly.

Stir the ingredients for a few minutes and then turn onto a plate. When cold, form into round flat cakes.

Brush over with remaining egg, cover with breadcrumbs and fry in hot fat until lightly browned.

(Submitted by Miss I. Bunting)

HADDOCK AND CHEESE PATTIES

6 oz Finnian Haddock
2 oz cheese
1 egg
6 oz short crust pastry
salt and pepper
white sauce

Cut pastry into rounds. Cook haddock in milk and use liquor for making sauce. Add cheese and chopped hard-boiled egg to sauce, place a dessertspoonful on each round of pastry, cover with another round of pastry. Brush with beaten egg and bake.

(Submitted by Mrs. Armitage, Locke Avenue)

MOCK CAVIARE

6 washed and boned anchovies
1 tsp dried parsley
pinch of cayenne
pinch of salt
squeeze of lemon juice
olive oil
clove of garlic

In a basin rubbed twice with a clove of garlic, or onion, pound the anchovies, add rest of ingredients and enough olive oil to make a smooth paste. Spread on dry biscuits,

(Submitted by Mrs. Frank Dennis)

MOCK CRAB SALAD

½ any cold white fish
1 tsp anchovy essence

Flake fish finely. Add essence. Put in centre of glass or silver entrée dish. Arrange nice salad around it.

(Submitted by the Matron and Staff of St. Helen's Hospital)

MOCK GOOSE

1 medium-sized onion, parboiled
1 lb mashed potatoes
apple sauce
sage, pepper and salt

Skin the sausages and break up with a fork. Put alternate layers of sausage and potatoes, seasoned with chopped onion, sage, pepper and salt, in a fairly hot oven till brown. Serve with apple sauce.

(Submitted by Mrs. H E. Bunting)

MOCK GROUSE

Put a fresh herring inside a pigeon before seasoning. Remove the herring and any bits of it that may have become detached, before serving. Serve with good brown sauce, flavoured with Port.

(Submitted by the Countess of Wharncliffe)

RED PIE

Quickly made and needs no rationed foodstuffs. Cut a tin of corned beef into slices and arrange them alternately with slices of tomato and seasoning, into a pie dish.

Sprinkle the top with potato risps and place in the oven to get thoroughly hot.

(Submitted by Viscountess Allendale)

SALMON LOAF

1 tin of salmon
¼ pint milk
2 oz breadcrumbs
2 eggs
little lemon rind

Flake the salmon, mix crumbs and lemon rind, a little salt and pepper. Add the beaten egg and milk, place in a greased loaf tin and press well down. Bake 30-45 minutes.

(Submitted by Mrs. Armitage Locke Avenue)

STEAMED SALMON MOULD

2 Tbsp rice
½ tin of salmon
1 egg
¼ pint parsley sauce
salt and pepper

Cook the rice until tender, add salmon, the beaten egg and parsley sauce, salt and pepper.

Put in a greased basin, cover with a greaseproof paper and steam for two hours.

(Submitted by Mrs. Bull Beechurst)

CURIOSITIES FROM BYGONE DAYS

The Roman invasion of Britain in AD 43 heralded the introduction of a number of new foods: game such as pheasants, peacocks and fallow deer; fruit and nuts such as grapes, figs, walnuts and mulberries; herbs such as parsley, borage, coriander, dill, mint, thyme, garlic; onion and sage; and vegetables such as cabbage, lettuce, turnip and mallow.

Shellfish such as oysters, cockles, whelks and scallops and sea fish such as cod, haddock and herring were also prized. On occasion, their menus were extravagant to the extreme such as one that included ostrich brains, peas mixed with grains of gold and lentils with precious stones.

By Medieval Times, bread had become Britain's staple food, although the quality of the bread depended on one's income. Wheat was reserved for the most wealthy, mixed wheat and rye flour was for the common people and in the cold and wet North, barley and other oats were used. Fish was equally important, especially during those time of the year when meat, eggs and dairy foods were banned by the Roman Catholic Church.

Ordinary people ate salted or pickled herring and dried cod and, in the summer months, river fish such as eels. Nobles and the wealthy had their choice of seals, sturgeons and porpoises from the sea and salmon, trout and carp as luxury fish from their own estates. Also, in order to get around the meat restrictions, some animals such as puffins were classified as fish because they were said to come from the sea and beavers that were said to have fish tails. Meat included pork, beef, mutton, goat, rabbit and hare; poultry included such unusual selections as swan, bustard, crane, heron, blackbirds and small birds such as thrushes and greenfinches.

Today, although some of us might still enjoy snails, frogs' legs, beaver tails, kangaroo and ostrich steaks, suckling pig and other such tasties, a growing concern with the protection of endangered species has fortunately eradicated bears' paws and similar foods from our menus. As to brews of eyes of newt and toads... the least said, the better.

Magdalena Gorrell Guimaraens

BEARS PAWS RUSS FASHION
Tana Willis Johnson, Gloucestershire
From a 1900s cookbook

"In Russia, bears paws are sold ready-skinned, as commonly, perhaps, as pigs' feet elsewhere. Although this is a dish little known in Central Europe, I very much doubt that it may yet be appetising for the people of the West."

Wash the bears' paws, wipe, salt and put them into a kitchen-basin; cover them with cooked marinade, and thus let them macerate for two or three days.

Spread a stewpan with trimmings of bacon and ham, and sliced vegetables: place the paws thereupon, moisten (covered) with their marinade and the broth, half-and-half, cover them with thin layers of bacon and boil them for seven or eight hours on a slow fire, adding more broth as the stock reduces.

The paws being tender, leave them in their stock till nearly cold; drain, wipe and divide each of them into four pieces lengthwise.

Sprinkle over cayenne pepper; roll them in melted lard, breadcrumbs, and broil them for half an hour on a very slow fire; then dish up.

Pour on the bottom of the dish some piquant sauce finished with two tablespoons of redcurrant jelly.

BEAVER TAIL AND BEANS
Elizabeth Ann Corner, B. C.

"While this dish might not be to everyone's taste nor be typical of today, beaver, which used to exist in Britain in ages past, may possibly have been prepared in a similar manner, although no doubt without the baked beans! Beaver meat, when properly prepared, is said to be similar in flavour to roast pork."

To remove skin from a beaver tail, blister it over very hot coals, let it cool and then pull the skin off. Cut into bite-sized pieces and mix into 6 cups of baked beans.

Add 1 chopped onion, 1 sliced carrot and ½ cup water. Cover and bake at 350°F for 2 hours.

PIG KILLING CAKE
Susan Cook, Westbank, B.C.

From "Through Yorkshire's Kitchen Door", Yorkshire Federation of Women's Institutes

"This cake was eaten warm on the day when a pig was killed. A party was usually held the same evening."

Make a short crust pastry with the addition of some currants and a little sugar. Roll out into flat cakes about 9 in across and 1in thick.

Bake till nicely brown then whilst still hot, split them open, spread with butter and sugar and a grating of nutmeg.

Sandwich the two halves together again and spread the top with butter, sugar and a little nutmeg.

CHRISTMAS PIE
Tana Willis Johnson, Gloucestershire

The following appeared in the Doncaster Gazette 17 January 1835.

"We are informed that Mrs. Kirk of the Old Ship Inn, Rotherham, has, with her accustomed liberality, provided for her friends, and especially for her Sheffield friends, a Christmas pie which, when taken to the oven, weighed upwards of seventeen stone.

It consists of one rump of beef, two legs of veal, two legs of pork, three hares, three couple of rabbits, three geese, two brace of pheasants, four brace of partridges, two turkeys, two couple of fowls, with 7 ½ stone of best flour.

We have no doubt that the good landlady of the Ship will be honoured with lots of visitors, not only to look at, but partake of, that extraordinary pie during Christmas."

POOR MAN'S GOOSE
Ann Scott, Bingley, West Yorkshire

From my Grandma's recipe book (ca. 1900). This came from Mrs Morritt, Guiseley, Leeds.

Take a deep dish, put a few pieces of dripping in the bottom, then a layer of sliced apples sprinkled with sugar; and upon that, a layer of sage and onion stuffing, then some slices of liver (lamb's) and a layer of raw sliced potatoes, and well sprinkled with salt. Repeat the layers again, untill the dish is full. Be sure to finish off with sliced potatoes. Dot with bits of dripping and bake for an hour in a moderate oven. Serve very hot.

ROOK PIE
Susan Cook, Westbank, B.C.

"The definition of a rook for this purpose is a young bird, recently left the nest and just able to fly. Available mid-May in North England."

SKINNING THE BIRDS
Cut the skin down the centre of the breast, draw the skin off in the direction of the wing, pulling it up to the first joint. Cut the wing at the joint and discard the end part.

Draw the skin from the legs and cut off at the shank joint. Cut the legs off at the joint where they join the body.

Insert your first finger at the breast cavity and wit one hand take hold of the lower portion of the neck with the other and pull apart. This will leave the breast in one hand and the remainder of the bird in the other. Discard this. Wash breast and legs well in cold water and rinse several times.

COOKING THE BIRDS
Stew breasts and legs gently until tender. (Improved if you add a small piece of steak a little beef dripping). When cool, remove the meat from the bones and place in a pie dish. Season well with salt and a sprinkle of cayenne pepper. Add a little gravy and cover wit short crust pastry. Bake until brown. Serve hot or cold with salad.

YORKSHIRE GOOSE PIE
Susan Cook, Westbank, B.C.

"This recipe for an "Economical Goose Pie" was copied from an early cookery book dated 1791 and dedicated to the Hon. Lady Wourton whom the author served as housekeeper."

Take a large fat goose, split it down the back and take all the bones out. De-bone a turkey and 2 ducks the same way. Season them very well with pepper and salt and with six woodcocks.

Lay the goose down on a clean dish with the skin side down and lay the turkey into the goose with the skin side down. Have ready a large Hare, cleaned well. Cut in pieces and put in the oven with 1 lb of butter; ¼ oz of mace, beaten fine; the same of white pepper and salt to your taste, till the meat will leave the bones, and scum the butter off the gravy. Pick the meat clean off and beat it with a marble mortar very fine with the butter you took off, and lay it in the turkey.

Take 24 lbs of the finest flour, 6 lbs of butter, ½ lb of rendered suet make the paste thick and raise the pie oval. Roll out a lump of paste and cut it in vine leaves or what form you will. Rub the pie with the yolks of eggs and put your ornaments on the walls, then turn your Hare, Turkey and Goose upside down and lay them in your pie with the ducks at each end and the woodcocks at the sides. Make your lid pretty thick and put it on. You may make flowers or the shape of folds in the paste on the lid, and make a hole in the middle of the lid. The walls of the pie are to be 1 ½ in thicker than the lid.

Rub it all over with the yolks of egg and bind it round with three-fold paper and lay the same over the top. It will take four hours baking in a brown bread oven.

When it comes out, melt 2 lbs of HistoHare and pour it hot into the pie through the hole. Close it up well and let it be for 8-10 days before you cut into it.

If you send it any distance close up the hole in the middle with cold butter to prevent the air from getting in.

FUNERAL BISCUITS
Susan Cook, Westbank, B.C.
Sponge cake type

3 eggs
½ lb flour
½ lb sugar (loaf, crushed)

Beat the eggs and sugar together for 20 min. Add flour, mix well and leave to stand for 1 hour. Drop in large teaspoonfuls on to pieces of greased greaseproof paper placed on a baking tray. Cook in a fairly hot over (375°F) till firm but not browned, The tops should remain sugary.

FUNERAL BISCUITS
Susan Cook, Westbank, B.C.
Shortbread Type

1 ½ lb flour
¾ lb butter
¾ lb sugar
1 egg

Rub the butter into the flour and add the sugar and beaten egg. Roll out and cut into rounds. Bake in a moderate oven for 30 minutes. When cold, cut in half and place the 2 pieces one on top of the other. Wrap up and seal.

HISTORICAL NOTE

FUNERAL BISCUITS

"In times past, one did not attend a funeral unless invited to do so, or had been 'bid' to attend. The children thought it a real occasion when they learned that their mother had been 'bid' because they knew that she would bring back with her the Funeral cakes for them to eat.

There were two kinds of Funeral Cakes. The first was of a spongy texture and was usually made by the bakers and sold in the village shop. The second type was more like a shortbread and this was made by the deceased's family and relations. Both kinds of cakes were round in shape and when cold were cut in half, one half being placed on top of the other. Each pair of halves was then wrapped up in a special way in unwaxed paper; and sealed with black sealing wax. Whilst the mourners were waiting for the cortège to come out of the house, two women dressed in deepest black would circulate outside the house, one distributing Funeral cakes and the other, glasses of wine.

A Funeral biscuit wrapper printed in York in the year 1846 uses a sentimental lament as its central motive The verses are enclosed in a diamond shaped frame and it in its turn is surrounded by a four-lined verse. The wrapper is bordered by a continuous scroll design, the whole being printed in deepest black. A space is left for the name of the deceased, together with the date of his (or her) demise."

In Through the Yorkshire's Kitchen Door
Ed. The Yorkshire Federation of Women's Institutes, 1957

HINTS FOR THE HOMEMAKER

CURE FOR LOW SPIRITS
Anonymous, 1900

Take 1 oz of the seeds of Resolution properly mixed with the oil of Good Conscience. Infuse into it a large spoonful of the Balsam of Patience. Distil carefully a composing plant called Others' Woes, which you will find in every part of the Garden of Life

Gather a handful of the blossoms of Hope, sweeten them with a syrup made of the Balm of Providence and if you can get any seeds of True Friendship, you will have a valuable medicine, but be careful not to add a weed called "Self-Interest" which will spoil the composition.

These ingredients well mixed and faithfully taken, will complete the cure.

"Keep an apple in the cake box to prevent cakes going dry but discard it when it's withered and another one supply."

ON CHOOSING AND HANGING MEAT

Home-killed pork or mutton should hang for 5-7 days depending on the weather. Except for meat which is eaten slightly high, all meat and poultry should be hung head downwards and used sweet. If meat becomes slightly tainted, wash or soak it for a while in vinegar and water before cooking.

ON CLOTTED CREAM (1)

Clotted cream is not cheese. It's cream. I've watched my mother-in-law's twin sister (she's a farmer's wife) make it, but I've forgotten how. I think it's like this:

Take one (or several) cow(s)' milk and put into a tin basin. Put basin in dairy and

"Lamb chops if dipped in lemon juice before they're to be fried are really so delicious you'll want them multiplied."

leave for a day or two, until the milk and the fat separate. The fat rises to the top and can be lifted off to make cheese or butter. If you don't make cheese or butter with it, that's clotted cream!

Renia Simmonds

ON CLOTTED CREAM (2)

The old-fashioned, unpasteurised, now outlawed on health grounds, clotted cream is preferable. To explain the difference between the old ad the new, modern clotted cream is of a even consistency, whereas proper clotted cream has a thick yellow crust on top, the clots (or lumps) under it, and the thin is at the bottom.

Terry Leatman, Torquay, Devon

ON CURDS AND WHEY

When you separate milk, curds is the solid, whey is the liquid. You can curdle full cream milk by heating and adding a little lemon whilst stirring. Then make your Yorkshire Curd Tart!

TO BOTTLE GREEN PEAS

Fill the bottles which must be clean and sound, as full as possible with fresh gathered peas, and cork them. Put the bottles in a saucepan of cold water up to their necks, put the cover on the pan, let the water boil up and keep it boiling, adding more water if it boils away, for two hours.

Let the bottles cook in the water then take them out ad dip the corks in sealing wax or resin. Keep them in a cool place. Peas should be bottled when in the greatest perfection.

Martyn Gleaden, Wath-Upon-Dearne
[From a 1900 notebook by Mary Duckett]

REGARDING ALUMINIUM PANS

Aluminium pans should never be washed in water containing soda as this will damage the metal. If you boil eggs in an aluminium pan, it will turn black and be particularly difficult to clean. To avoid this, add a little vinegar to the water.

ON WASHING BONE-HANDLED CUTLERY

Anyone fortunate to be given a set of old Sheffield knives with bone handles must take care in washing them so that they do not become unglued and loose.

Take a jug, fill it up with just enough warm, not too hot, soapy water to cover the blades and place the knives in to soak, handles up. Leave a while, rinse and dry with a soft cloth.

A little baking soda in the water helps. Rubbing the blades with a little dry mustard or scouring powder also helps to remove stubborn stains.

ON REMOVING STAINS FROM TEA CUPS

Dip a slice of lemon in salt and rub on inside of tea cups to remove stains.

FURNITURE POLISH
Kathleen Allott Guimaraens
ex-Rotherham, in Northern Portugal

1 cup turpentine
Add:
1 cup meths and shake
Add:
1 cup raw linseed oil and shake.

Shake well before use. For varnished, painted, waxed or other surfaces.

TO PRESERVE LEAVES
Ann Collier, Wentworth

First slit the stems of the branches whose leaves you wish to preserve. Place in warm water and allow to stand for some hours. (Leaves that are severed from the branch will curl up.)

Remove from water and stand in a solution of 1 part glycerine to 2 parts boiling water. The branches only need to stand in a couple of inches of this solution, so choose a narrow vessel. Best done in August.

Domestic Economy 1898
Extracted from the *Sunlight Year Book for 1898*
by Brenda Griffiths

Domestic Economy

There are a thousand-and-one methods by which a careful and thoughtful housewife may economise, without being stingy. The great point is that she should regard it as her business in life to make the best of her home – as much her business as it is that of her husband's to pursue his avocation – and the battle is won. She will soon find out by experience what to do and what to avoid.

Some advice

Butter

When butter is very dear, good meat-dripping may be used in its stead. Good dripping, in fact, is much better than bad butter and with a trifle of salt sprinkled over it when spread on the bread, most children will eat it gladly. It is very useful as a heat-giver to the body, being, in fact, wholesome food.

Eggs

Eggs are also good food, but when boiled hard, the white is indigestible. They should be lightly cooked. Perhaps they are most digestible when beaten up in a cup of freshly made good tea. Even a stale egg – not too stale, may be taken in this way. A cup of tea thus fortified is very good for persons in a weakly state of health, and may be taken with a slice or two of bread and butter. As to the economy of eggs, the price varies so much that it is difficult to give a decided opinion; perhaps the best guide is this: they cease to be really economical when they cost over a penny each.

Tea

Tea varies immensely and so do opinions about this valuable beverage. Flat, washy tea is bad; very strong tea is bad also; but tea freshly-made brisk tea is distinctly beneficial. Very few people seem to make tea properly. The cardinal point is to use fresh water; freshly boiled, and to use it directly it does boil, but to see that it boils; the steam should jet out vigourously from the kettle spout. The reason for this is obvious; water boiled up twice becomes flat, and the point is to use it just as it is bubbling and effervescing with its first boiling.

Then the teapot should be made quite warm before the tea is put into it; and all the boiling water for the tea should be poured on at once; in other words if you have sufficient tea in the pot fill it up at once. Tea should never be warmed twice. Warren Hastings, our great Indian pro-consul, who may be supposed to have learned of the value of tea in the East, never would permit this.

As for the quantity, a teaspoonful for each person and one for the pot, is a rough-and-ready rule which seems to work well. When the water is pourd on, place the teapot near the fire for about five minutes or so, the point being to keep the water very hot, but not boiling, and not to stew the leaves a long time, otherwise the tannin may be extracted, which is indigestible. If there is no fireplace, place a cosey (sic) over the teapot after making the tea. After use, the tea-leaves should be removed from the pot at once and the teapot washed and dried.

These details may be thought trivial but they cause all the difference between good and bad tea, and while the one in moderation is beneficial to the system, the other is pernicious. Used tea-leaves may be sprinkled over the carpet when sweeping it, to help in laying the dust, and finally they may be burned. Should live animals be kept a few may be given to them.

Alcoholic Drinks

As a rule these are not necessary to health and are usually injurious, consequently they are not econonical. People should avoid contracting the habit of drinking, whether alcoholic or other beverages. Too much fluid in the stomach produces ill-health. A certain exception may perhaps be made in favour of milk, because milk is such a nutritious food, but much fruit and many vegetables contain fluid in themselves.

The body of course needs fluidm but there is all the difference between drinking to supply the healthy needs of the body and drinking for the sake of habit, even if the drink be non-alcoholic. It is the drink-habit as wasteful, uneconomical and positively unhealthy, that we are now denouncing.

An enormous amount of money is annually wasted in drinks of various kinds thata would buy better food, better clothes, better furniture, better books, better everything in short, and more of it.

Remember then to avoid over-driig even at meals; it is distinctly unhealthy, as it lowers the tone of and disorders the stomach; even too long a draught of water is bad, but as a rule the temptation to drink too much water seldom arises.

REMEDIES

CAUTION

The following 'home cures' are ABSOLUTELY NOT recommended to you as suitable remedies to be used today. Our ancestors were very ingenious in caring for their families under varying circumstances. One problem was that our ancestors may not have had doctors living in their vicinities. Whilst word was being sent, perhaps by horse and buggy, the old model cars or worse, by shank's poney, to ask the doctor to make a house call (remember them?!), some temporary relief had to be administered. We can only admire the methods they used, even if in some cases these 'cures' sound worse than the illness!

Another problem was the economic factor. The level of poverty of the majority prevented nany for asking for a doctor's services, even if one were in the vicinity. Again, please proceed with extreme caution if you are tempted to get creative!

June Ridsdale

ACHES, PAINS & SORES

FOR ACHES & PAINS

4 oz paraffin
4 oz methylated spirits
4 oz white wine vinegar
1 oz camphor
2 egg whites

Mix together, shake well. Rub sore spots.

EMBROCATION

2 oz olive oil
1 oz oil of amber
1 drachm oil of cloves

To be mixed together and rubbed on the chest at bedtime.

FOR BURNS OR SCALDS

Get a raw egg. Crack open and quickly cover the affected area with the white of the egg.

As soon as relief is obtained, peel the thin skin that lines the inside of the eggshell and place over the affected area. Let dry.

If done quickly, you will have no pain and little or no blistering.

Note: This remedy actually works and is very, very effective There is some property in the egg white that cools down the skin. The thin skin from the eggshell helps keep the burnt area clean and disinfected. I've used it myself.

Magdalena

FOR TOOTHACHE

Get a piece of sheet zinc, about the size of a sixpence, and a piece of silver, say a teaspoon. Place them together and place the aching tooth either in between or next to then. In a few minutes the pain will disappear.

FOR RHEUMATISM

2 oz flowers of sulpha
2 oz epson salts
2 oz citrate of magnesium
1 oz ginger

Take a teaspoonful in a glass of milk.

GREEN OINTMENT FOR SORES, CUTS & BURNS

4-penny tin of eucalyptus
2-penny tin of vaseline
3 pennyworth of oil of swallow
¼ oz shredded bees wax

Put all in a jar, stand in boiling water, on fire. Stir with wooden spon until dissolved and put in small pots and jars.

COUGHS & SNEEZES

MIS BISAT'S ASTHMA CURE
Martyn Gleaden, Wath-Upon-Dearne
From a 1900 notebook by Mark Duckett

½ oz chloric ether
½ oz oxynel squills
½ oz paregoric

Put the above in an 8oz medicine bottle and fill up with cold water. Take a tablespoon three times a day.

FOR CHILDREN'S COUGHS
Beverley Ramsden, Renfrew, Ontario

1 small teacup of black treacle. Add a small piece of fresh butter about the size of ½ a hen's egg, 3 Tbsp demarara sugar, 1 tsp olive oil and 2 Tbsp best vinegar.

Keep warm by the fire and give 2 tsp before bedtime.

COUGH MIXTURE (1)
Beverley Ramsden, Renfrew, Ontario

2 drachms peppermint
2 drachms aniseed
2 drachms laudenum
2 drachms ether
½ lb black treacle

Scald black treacle with 1 pint of water. Cool. Add drugs and flavourings.

Dose: 1 Tbsp 3 times a day.

COUGH MIXTURE (2)
Beverley Ramsden, Renfrew, Ontario

2 oz cod liver oil
2 oz glycerine
2 oz honey
juice of 3 lemons

Dose: 1 tsp for children
1 dessertspoon for adults

COUGH MIXTURE (3)
Andrew Talbot Hopkinson

"I found the following cough syrup recipe in my grandmother's recipe book. Laudanum was not a banned substance in her young days. My grandparents lived in Doncaster."

1 dram white wine vinegar
1 dram spirits of ether
1 dram oil of peppermint
1 dram oil of aniseed
1 dram syrup of squills
½ lb black treacle
1 dram ipecacuana wine
1 dram Spanish juice (liquorice)
1 dram laudanum
1 ½ pints water

Boil Spanish juice and dreacle in the water to one pint, When cold add other ingredients.

Dose: 2 Tbsp full 3 times a day.

COUGHS & SORE THROATS

Warm 6 oz pure honey until it liquifies. Stir into 6 oz white wine vinegar. Put in wide-mouthed bottle and cork well.

CURE FOR STUBBORN COLDS
Beverley Ramsden, Renfrew, Ontario

5 lb elderberries simmered with 1 lb white sugar.
Strain.
1 Tbsp in hot water will cure the ost stubborn cold.

INFLUENZA MIXTURE
Beverley Ramsden, Renfrew, Ontario

½ oz paregoric
½ oz sweet nitre
¼ oz sal volatile
¼ oz spirits of chloroform
½ oz syrup of squills
Make up to 16 oz with water.

Dose; 1 Tbsp 3 times a day.

INTERNAL COMPLAINTS

FOR WIND AT HEART

2 drachms sal volatile
2 drachms tincture of gentian
2 drachms chloric ether

Fill medicine bottle with above ingredients and fill up with water.

Dose: 2 Tbsp as required

FOR CONSTIPATION

1 lb prunes
½ demarara sugar
2 oz powdered senna
1 oz powdered ginger
2 Tbsp brandy

Stew prunes in a very little water until soft. Sieve.
   Add sugar while hot and when cold, add other ingredients.
   Mix thoroughly.

Note: A squill is a bulb of the lily family, used since Ancient Greece as a medical ingredient, especially to treat asthma and coughs. It is highly toxic.   ***Magdalena***

SKIN DISORDERS

Albert Harrand's Home-Made
SALVE FOR BOILS
Martyn Gleaden, Wath-Upon-Dearne
From a 1900 notebook by Mark Duckett

¼ lb mutton suet of the loin
3 oz butter without salt
3 oz powdered rozen
1 ½ oz ees wax

Mix buttr, suet and wax, Stir in rozen and stir till all is dissolved. Strain, put in egg cups and turn out when cold.

ECZEMA

In a quart bottle, put the strained juice of 3 lemons. 2 oz epsom solts and 3 Tbsp of pure liquid honey. Fill up bottle with hot water.

Dose: Drink a wine glass full, 3 times a day

WARTS

Choose the most perfect apple you can find. Count the number of warts and cut the apple carefully into as many pieces as there are warts. Rub the warts with the apple taking care not to damage the fruit.

Carefully reassemble the apple, tie with string to hold the pieces in place and bury ib te ground. As the apple rots, the warts will fall off, never to reappear.

Note: As strange as it may seem, this remedy was also applied by a 'faith healer/white witch' in Portugal, years ago, to my young daughter whose hands and knees were covered with warts that resisted all conventional medical attempts to remove them. It worked a treat and the warts disappeared, never to reappear. Several years later, a friend went to the same healer who also resorted to this treatment for her son, with the same excellent result! *Magdalena*

PERSONAL HYGIENE

HAIR TONIC

1 oz spirit of turpentine
1 oz Trotter's oil
30 drops of acetic solution of cantharides

Apply a little to the roots of the hair, 2-3 times a week.

Note: Trotter's oil is an oil obtained by boiling down sheep and pig's feet.

Cantharides are blister beetles. Also used as an aphrodisiac, known as Spanish fly. ***Magdalena***

INDEX

			Page
Bacon Duff			70
Beverages			
	Beer – Country Scout		27
	– Gayle Beer		27
	– Ginger Beer		27
	– Mild Country Ale		27
	– Mulled Ale		28
	Bishop		23
	Bishop's Night Cap		23
	Black or White Eldeberry Wine		30
	Bookham Cream		23
	Champagne & Brandy Punch		29
	Champagne Cup		29
	Egg Nog		23
	Elderflower Champagne 1		29
	Elderflower Champagne 2		29
	Elderflower Cordial		30
	Hot Punch		24
	Hot Punch Tea		24
	Loving Cup		24
	Mulled Wine		28
	Negus		24
	Pope's Posset		24
	Pink Port Summer Cocktail		25
	Port Wine & Tonic Cocktail		25
	Potato Wine		30
	Rum Toddy		25
	Sloe Gin		25
	Turnip Wine		31
	Yorkshire Beetroot Wine		31
Brains	Fried		70
	On Toast		70
Brawn	Brawn 1		70
	Brawn 2		71
	Chicken		71
	Cow heel and Beef		71
	Kangaroo Tail and Pig's Head		72
	Ox Cheek		72

	Pig's Head and Feet	72
	Pork a	72
	Pork b	73
	Pork c	73
	Sheep's Head	73
Bread	Currant, Wartime	87
	Date, Wartime	87
	Flat	17
	Fruited Brown, Wartime	88
	Fruited Loaves, Wartime	88
	Ginger, Wartime	88
	Harvo	88
	Hot Cross Buns, Wartime	88
	Loys' European	17
	Malt	17
	Malt, Wartime	89
	Mother's	17
	North Riding Yorkshire	17
	Plum Loaf, Wartime	89
	Spice Loaf, Wartime	89
	Vinegar Loaf	19
	Walnut	18
	York Mayne	19
Cakes & Biscruits	Apple Charlotte	33
	Brandy Snaps	11
	Bury Simnel	34
	Cream Cracker Biscuits	11
	Crumpets	11
	Elsie's Fruit Cake	34
	Fat Rascals Wartime	34
	Fat Rascal Turf Cakes	35
	Funeral Biscuits	96
	Ginger Biscuits	12
	Isabel Hardaker's Cake	35
	Lardy or Fatty Cake 1	35
	Lardy or Fatty Cake 2	35
	Non-sweet Tea Cakes	12
	Ormskirk Gingerbread	12
	Pig Killing Cake	95
	Potato Cakes	13
	Queen Cakes	38
	Ripon Apple Cake	33
	Sad Cakes	38
	Victoria Sponge Sandwich	39

Chutney	Green Apple	57
Curiosities From Bygone Days		93
Desserts	Banofee Pie	33
	Yorkshire Curd Cheesecake	34
	Curd Tart	34
	Eskimo Pie	34
	Lemon Cheesecake	36
	Lemon Sweet	66
	Sweet Suet Dumplings	66
	Yorkshire Curd Tart	38
Eggs	Pickled	74
	Russian Egg Dish	91
Fish	Fish Cakes, Wartime	91
	Fried in Batter	41
	Fish and Potato Puff	41
	Fish Paste	42
	Fishcakes or Rissoles	41
	Good Friday Fish Pie	42
	Haddock & Cheese Patties, Wartime	91
	Mock Caviare, Wartime	91
	Mock Crab Salad, Wartime	91
	Mrs. Cheadle's Salmon Paste	42
	Salmon Loaf	42
	Salmon Loaf, Wartime	92
	Steamed Salmon Mould, Wartime	92
	Stuffed Plaice	42
	Whitebait	43
	Yorkshire Herring Pie	43
Hints for the Homemaker		99
Meat	Bacon and Cow Heel Pudding	53
	Bacon and Cow Heel Mould	53
	Bag	53
	Bear Paws Russian Fashion	94
	Beaver Tail and Beans	94
	Beef and Cow Heel Mould	53
	Boiled Salted Beef and Dumplings	45
	Bradford Hash	45
	Cow Heel or Ox-Feet, Fried	54
	Cow Heel, Boiled	54
	Faggots or Savoury Ducks	45
	Hare, How to jug	47
	Hot Meat Salad, Wartime	90
	Mock Goose, Wartime	92

	Mock Grouse, Wartime	92
	Ox Cheek, Stewed	55
	Poor Man's Goose	95
	Steak and Kidney Pudding	49
	Toad in the Hole	49
	Veal Birds with Raisin Stuffing	51
Meat Pies	Christmas Pie	94
	Cow Heel Pasty	54
	Pork Pie 1	48
	Pork Pie 2	48
	Pork Pie, Small Victorian Raised	49
	Red Pie, Wartime	92
	Rook Pie, Wartime	95
	Victorian Christmas Pie	46
	Victorian Yorkshire Pie	51
	Yorkshire Goose Pie	95
Parkin	About Yorkshire Parkin	14
	Parkin 1	13
	Parkin 2	13
	Parkin 3	13
	Parkin 4	14
	Yorkshire Wartime	90
Paté and Potted Liver Paste		47
Peas	Fritters, Wartime	90
	Mushy	74
	Pease Pudding	74
Pickles and Sauces		
	Brown Gravy	57
	Green Apple Chutney	57
	Horseradish	58
	Mint and Cucumber Sauce for Lamb	58
	Piccalilli	57
	Yorkshire Relish	57
Porridge	Milk Porridge	21
	Serving suggestions	21
Preserves	Apple, Plum or Greengage Jam	59
	Blanket Jam	59
	Bruce's Jam-making Made Easy	60
	Gooseberry Jam	60
	Lemon Curd 1	60
	Lemon Curd 2	60
	Marmalade	61

	Plum Jam	61
	Quinces	62
	Victorian Apple Jam	61
Puddings	Baked Suet	63
	Bakewell	63
	Batter Pudding with Apples	63
	Bread	63
	Bread & Butter	64
	Deb's Suet Pudding	64
	Delaware	64
	Fruit	65
	Fruit, Steak & Kidney	65
	Golden	65
	Mrs. Barnes' Carrot	66
	Puzzle	67
	Roly Poly 1	67
	Roly Poly 2	67
	Rol Poly Microwave	67
	Savoury Suet Pudding	75
	Seasoned Suet Pudding	74
	Sultana	68
	Yorkshire Savoury	75
Remedies from the Past		103
Scones	Brown	15
	Currant Tea	15
	Great Grandad's	15
	Griddle	16
	Plain	16
	Tea	16
Soup	Carrot and Leek	77
	Cow Heel	78
	Cream of Chicken	77
	Homemade Chicken	77
	Lettuce or Cabbage	77
	Suggestions	78
Spanish or Liquorice		82
	Pontefract or Pomfret Cakes	82
Suet	Crust Pastry	48
	Dumplings for Stews	75
Sweets	Cherry Walnut Divinity	79
	Chocolate Coating for Toffee	81
	Coconut Ice	79

	Divinity	79
	Homemade Yorkshire Humbugs	80
	Honeycomb Toffee	80
	Plot or Bonfire Toffee	81
	Strawberry Divinity Fudge	80
	Tom Trot	81
	Treacle Toffee 1	81
	Treacle Toffee 2	81
Tarts	Maids of Honour 1	36
	Maids of Honour 2	36
	Maids of Honour 3	36
	Maids of Honour, Wartime	89
	Stamford Bridge Spear Pies	39
Tips for Roasting Meat		
	Timetable for Roasting Fresh Meat	56
	Tips for Roasting a Standing Beef Rib	55
Tripe	How to dress tripe	50
	Braised	50
	Raw	50
	Stuffed	51
	Tripe Pie	50
	With Milk and Onions	51
Wartime Tasties		87
WEIGHTS & MEASURES		113
Yorkshire Pudding		
	Granny's, with Onions	84
	Mrs. Beeton's	84
	Savoury	85
	Seasoned	85
	Yorkshire Pudding 1	85
	Yorkshire Pudding 2	86
	Yorkshire Pudding 3	87

WEIGHTS & MEASURES

FOR OLD-FASHIONED RECIPES, EQUIVALENTS FOR WEIGHTS:
¼ oz = 1 copper threepenny bit
½ oz = 1 penny and 1 halfpenny
1 oz = 3 new pennies

NOTE that Europeans tend to use separate measures for liquid and dry ingredients, whereas Americans and Canadians use standards cups as a rule for both. European tablespoons tend to measure slightly more than American ones.

DRY WEIGHT MEASURE EQUIVALENTS
OUNCES>GRAMS and GRAMS > OUNCES
POUNDS > KILOS and KILOS > POUNDS

OUNCES > GRAMS		GRAMS > OUNCES		POUNDS > KILOS		KILOS > POUNDS	
1	30	1	0.035	1	0.454	1	2.2
2	60	30	1	2	0.91	2	4.4
4	115	100	3.5	3	1.36	3	6.6
8	230	125	4 ½	4	2.27	5	11

LIQUID MEASURE EQUIVALENTS
CUPS>FLUID OZ>TBSP>TSP>MILLILITRE

CUP	FLUID OZ	TBSP	TSP	MILLILITRE
1	8	16	48	237
¾	6	12	36	177
2/3	5	11	32	158
½	4	8	24	118
1/3	3	5	16	79
¼	2	4	12	59
1/8	1	2	6	30
1/16	5	1	3	15

APPROXIMATE TIN (CAN) SIZES

WEIGHT	CONTENT IN CUPS
6 ounces	¾ cup
8 ounces	1 cup

NOTES

Printed in Great Britain
by Amazon